Frontispiece
Peer Gynt (2005).
Photograph
by Lesley
Leslie-Spinks,
courtesy of Lesley
Leslie-Spinks

ROBERT WILSON

Routledge Performance Practitioners is a series of introductory guides to the key theatre-makers of the last century. Each volume explains the background to and the work of one of the major influences on twentieth- and twenty-first-century performance.

Robert Wilson is an American–European director who is also a performer, installation artist, writer, designer of light and much more besides – a crossover polymath who dissolves both generic and geographical boundaries and is a precursor of globalisation in the arts. This is the first book to combine:

- analysis of his main productions, situated in their American and European socio-cultural and political contexts
- an exploration of his 'visual book', workshop and rehearsal methods, and collaborative procedures
- a study of his aesthetic principles and the elements of composition that distinguish his directorial approach
- a series of practical exercises for students and practitioners highlighting Wilson's technique.

As a first step towards critical understanding, and as an initial exploration before going on to further, primary research, **Routledge Performance Practitioners** are unbeatable value for today's student.

Maria Shevtsova is Professor of Drama and Theatre Arts at Goldsmiths College, University of London. She is author of *Dodin and the Maly Drama Theatre: Process to Performance* (Routledge, 2004) and co-editor of *Fifty Key Theatre Directors* (Routledge, 2005).

ROUTLEDGE PERFORMANCE PRACTITIONERS

Series editor: Franc Chamberlain, University College Cork

Routledge Performance Practitioners is an innovative series of introductory handbooks on key figures in twentieth-century performance practice. Each volume focuses on a theatre-maker whose practical and theoretical work has in some way transformed the way we understand theatre and performance. The books are carefully structured to enable the reader to gain a good grasp of the fundamental elements underpinning each practitioner's work. They will provide an inspiring springboard for future study, unpacking and explaining what can initially seem daunting.

The main sections of each book cover:

- personal biography
- explanation of key writings
- description of significant productions
- reproduction of practical exercises.

Volumes currently available in the series are:

Eugenio Barba by Jane Turner
Augusto Boal by Frances Babbage
Michael Chekhov by Franc Chamberlain
Jacques Copeau by Mark Evans
Etienne Decroux by Thomas Leabhart
Jerzy Grotowski by James Slowiak and Jairo Cuesta
Anna Halprin by Libby Worth and Helen Poyner
Jacques Lecoq by Simon Murray
Joan Littlewood by Nadine Holdsworth
Vsevolod Meyerhold by Jonathan Pitches
Ariane Mnouchkine by Judith Miller
Konstantin Stanislavsky by Bella Merlin

Hijikata Tatsumi and Ohno Kazuo by Sondra Horton Fraleigh and
    Tamah Nakamura
Robert Wilson by Maria Shevtsova

Future volumes will include:

Antonin Artaud
Pina Bausch
Bertolt Brecht
Peter Brook
Rudolf Laban
Robert Lepage
Lee Strasberg
Mary Wigman

ROBERT WILSON

Maria Shevtsova

LONDON AND NEW YORK

First published 2007
by Routledge
2 Park Square, Milton Park, Abingdon, Oxon OX14 4RN

Simultaneously published in the USA and Canada
by Routledge
270 Madison Ave, New York, NY 10016

Routledge is an imprint of the Taylor & Francis Group,
an informa business

Typeset in Perpetua by
Newgen Imaging Systems (P) Ltd, Chennai, India
Printed and bound in Great Britain by
Antony Rowe Ltd, Chippenham, Wiltshire

British Library Cataloguing in Publication Data
A catalogue record for this book is available from
the British Library

Library of Congress Cataloging in Publication Data
Shevtsova, Maria, 1945–
    Robert Wilson / by Maria Shevtsova.
        p. cm. – (Routledge performance practitioners)
    Includes bibliographical references and index.
      1. Wilson, Robert, 1941 – Criticism and interpretation. I. Title.
    PN2287.W494S45   2007
    792.023'3092–dc22   2006032640

ISBN10: 0–415–33880–8 (hbk)
ISBN10: 0–415–33881–6 (pbk)
ISBN10: 0–203–44845–6 (ebk)

ISBN13: 978–0–415–33880–6 (hbk)
ISBN13: 978–0–415–33881–3 (pbk)
ISBN13: 978–0–203–44845–8 (ebk)

FOR SASHA

CONTENTS

List of figures xi
Acknowledgements xiii

1 A WORKING LIFE **1**

 Becoming Robert Wilson 1
 Dance plays, silent operas and words 7
 Art and politics: the 1960s and after 14
 Wilson after *Einstein* 26

2 METHOD, ELEMENTS AND PRINCIPLES **41**

 A workshop method 42
 Elements and principles 52

3 *EINSTEIN ON THE BEACH* **83**

 Itinerary and reception 83
 Einstein on the Beach: a landmark 88
 Structure and form 89
 Breakdown of the work 92
 Summing up 112

4   PRACTICAL EXERCISES   **119**

Movement 121
Body imaging 129
Make-up 131
Composing a silent play 132
Sound and music 133
Working with texts 142
Light 151

A short glossary of terms   **153**
Bibliography   **157**
Index   **165**

FIGURES

1.1   *Deafman Glance* (1971). Photograph by R. Nusimovici   8
1.2   *KA MOUNTAIN and GUARDenia TERRACE* (1972).
      Photograph by Bahman Djalali   11
1.3   *Death Destruction and Detroit* (1979).
      Photograph by Ruth Walz   28
1.4   *Hamlet: a monologue* (1995). Photograph
      by T. Charles Erickson   34
2.1   *I La Galigo* (2004). Photograph by Pavel Antonov   44
2.2   *I La Galigo* (2004). Photograph by
      Kim Cheong and Ung Ruey Loon   45
2.3   *Peer Gynt* (2005). Photograph by
      Lesley Leslie-Spinks   55
2.4   *Les Fables de la Fontaine* (2004). Photograph
      by Martine Franck   61
2.5   *Peer Gynt* (2005). Photograph by
      Lesley Leslie-Spinks   62
2.6   *The Black Rider* (1990). Photograph by
      Clärchen Baus-Mattar   66
2.7   *Woyzeck* (2000). Photograph by
      Erik Hansen-Hansen   69
2.8   *Peer Gynt* (2005). Photograph by
      Lesley Leslie-Spinks   75

2.9   *Woyzeck* (2000). Photograph by
      Erik Hansen-Hansen   79
2.10 *The Winter's Tale* (2005). Photograph by
      Lesley Leslie-Spinks   81
2.11 *Orlando* (1993). Photograph by
      Abisag Tüllman   82
3.1   *Einstein on the Beach* (1976). Photograph by
      Babette Mangolte   96
3.2   *Einstein on the Beach* (1976). Photograph by
      Babette Mangolte   101
3.3   *Einstein on the Beach* (1976). Photograph by
      Babette Mangolte   107
3.4   *Einstein on the Beach* (1976). Photograph by
      T. Charles Erickson [1992]   108
3.5   *Einstein on the Beach* (1976). Photograph by
      Babette Mangolte   110

ACKNOWLEDGEMENTS

I am deeply indebted to the Arts and Humanities Research Council for granting me both a Research Leave Award and a Small Grant in the Creative and Performing Arts, and to Goldsmiths College, University of London for honouring the Research Leave Award in kind. I am no less indebted to the British Academy for its Small Research Grant. The present volume could not have been completed without their support.

My sincere thanks go to Robert Wilson, his Assistant Director Ann-Christin Rommen and his assistants Christof Belka and Christoph Schletz for their generous attention and time; also, to all the staff at the Byrd Hoffman Water Mill Foundation and especially Jason Loeffler and Lisa Bennett for helping in all ways. Thank you Carsten Siebert and Kenji Troelstrup for your smiling support. My thanks to the New York Public Library for the Performing Arts and especially Sarah Ziebell Mann. To Frank Hentschker for a rendez-vous *manqué*. To Andrzej Wirth for bed and breakfast.

My research would not have been possible without the co-operation of theatres and their staff. I thank especially Det Norske Teatret and Ida Michaelsen, the Berliner Ensemble and Jutta Febers and the Barbican Centre in London. My warmest thanks to Monica Ohlsson and Lesley Leslie-Spinks for sharing their enthusiasm for Robert Wilson's work. Thank you Maggie Gibb, Rachel Shapiro, Patrice Pavis and David Williams.

I wish to thank all the photographers for their kind co-operation. Photographs courtesy of Lesley Leslie-Spinks for Figures 2.3, 2.5, 2.8, 2.10, Babette Mangolte for Figures 3.1, 3.2, 3.3, 3.5, Ruth Walz for Figure 1.3 and Clärchen Baus-Mattar for Figure 2.6. Photographs courtesy of Pavel Antonov for Figure 2.1 and T. Charles Erickson for Figures 1.4 and 3.4. Photographs courtesy of Esplanade Theatres on the Bay/Singapore and Change Performing Arts for Figure 2.2, Magnum Photos for Figure 2.4 and Hansen-Hansen.com for Figures 2.7 and 2.9.

All translations from the original French and Italian texts are by me [MS].

A WORKING LIFE

BECOMING ROBERT WILSON

Born in Waco, Texas, in 1941, Robert Wilson suffered from a speech impediment that was cured when he was 17 by Byrd Hoffman, a local teacher of dance. Wilson thinks of her as the first artist he had ever met. Byrd Hoffman, who was in her seventies, would play the piano in an adjoining room while he, free from her gaze, moved about whichever way he wished. As Wilson observes, she delivered him from his stutter by teaching him to release tension, to 'just relax' and let 'energy flow through so, so that I wasn't blocked' (quoted in Brecht, 1994: 14).

This event in the life of an adolescent who, he claims, had had a relatively lonely childhood was to leave its mark on Wilson's work in the theatre. Movement – idiosyncratic, 'Wilsonian' – was to become its fundamental principle and penetrate its every aspect so deeply – gesture, light, colour, costume, sound, word – that Wilson could credibly claim, even early in his career, that 'everything I do can be seen as dance' (Lesschaeve, 1977: 224). If the pioneer dancer and choreographer Martha Graham, whom Wilson admired, could assert that the body never lies (Copeland, 2004: 12), Wilson could be no less certain because of his own experience that the body speaking truthfully in movement was the way of physical and mental healing. The key was in letting it find its appropriate path. The freedom not to seek effects but just let be, which Wilson has always encouraged in his performers, arguably stems, at least in part, from this insight.

In 1959, Wilson enrolled in a business administration course at the University of Texas, probably to please his lawyer father who wanted conventional success for his son. He dropped out in 1962, just before he was to graduate (Brecht, 1994: 15), and spent some months studying painting with George McNeil, an American abstract expressionist painter in Paris. He returned to the United States, now to New York, as a student of architecture at Pratt Institute in Brooklyn. He allegedly had a nervous breakdown and attempted suicide (ibid.: 20), and graduated from Pratt in 1966. Wilson spent the summers of 1964 and 1965 in Texas continuing the theatre work with children that he had begun soon after finishing high school. He and the children wrote their scripts, performing in churches, construction sites, garages and vacant lots – anywhere that could be taken over as a performance space. The thing that most interested him, Wilson was to say in 1970, was 'education, teaching . . . it's like the biggest challenge' (ibid.: 22).

Graduation from Pratt was followed by Wilson's short apprenticeship to the anything-but-conventional architect Paolo Soleri in Arizona and, in 1967, by *Poles*, his first commissioned architectural work:

> In a broad flat field he erected 576 vertical telephone poles in a square array resembling an amphitheatre. Rising from a height of two-and-one-half feet to fourteen feet the incline created by the pole tops is attractive, accessible and human in scale. It offers precarious seats, an arena for some event or a jungle-gym for children at play.... Isolated from view except for visitors to the field, *Poles* inhabits its own landscape, a surreal image contradicting the natural site.
>
> (Stearns, 1984: 37)

It is clear from this account that Wilson's construction or 'architectural sculpture' (ibid.) was also a potential theatre and playground in one, a combination that may well have come to him from his making theatre in Texas with children. His work afterwards on a variety of stages across the world reflected a similarly architectural concern with building a space in which all play elements could be organised systematically. Many years later, Wilson would win the prize for sculpture at the 1993 Venice Biennale with an otherwise theatrical and 'surreal' work (the adjective would justifiably stick to Wilson throughout his career) that was actually an installation sculpture. This was *Memory/Loss*, which featured a mould of Wilson's head and shoulders in a large floor of cracked mud. Wilson's voice could be heard reading fragments of a text he had written, and was complemented by a soundscore by Hans Peter Kuhn who, by then, had become one of his regular collaborators.

Julia Kristeva, the renowned French theorist turned psychoanalyst, was on the jury hotly criticised for awarding the prize to Wilson for *sculpture*, the assumption being that the work did not fit the bill. Kristeva countered:

> But clearly the traditional categories – painting, sculpture, stagecraft, etc. – no longer correspond to reality. Personally, I think this is due to the crisis in our psychic space and the borders that separate the object and the subject. In the same way that there is a breaking down of the boundaries between objects, there is an intrication [*sic*] of the roles of the artist and the spectator, erasing the borders between the self and the other. This lack of differentiation can have a dramatic effect on some people: loss of sense of self, hallucinations, etc. But it can also give rise to jubilation, because it creates a sense of osmosis with Being, the Absolute.
>
> (Kristeva, 1994: 65)

Kristeva stresses that Wilson's abolition of established artistic categories obliges viewers to cross perceptual boundaries, which is a double-edge (even faintly psychotic) experience – both 'loss of sense of self' *and* 'jubilation'. For Wilson, however, cross-border perception, for creator and spectator alike, can only be positive since it calls upon unexercised dimensions of the imagination. This liberating power, while applicable to *Memory/Loss*, as to *Poles* and all his performance pieces, is at the heart of the matter: Wilson is a polymath – an architect, designer, painter, installation artist, writer, performer, director, and more – yet the diversity of his output is on a continuum. 'It's all part of one concern', Wilson states in response to criticism of his 2000 installation retrospective of fashion designer Giorgio Armani at the Guggenheim Museum in New York: 'many people . . . thought it should not be in a museum of "fine art"' (*The Guardian*, 11 September 2003). He no more thinks in hierarchical terms about his work (like 'fine' versus 'popular') than he does about it and his daily life: 'Now I'll go home and watch television. Now I have sex. Now I'm with my boyfriend. Now I go to work. I don't see it as separate' (*The Guardian*, 19 May 2001).

Wilson's involvement in performance gathered speed while he was at Pratt. Along with others he 'pitched in' to help choreographer Alwin Nikolais (Nikolais in Shyer, 1989: 290), designed the sets for Murray Louis's *Junk Dances* and made gigantic puppets for *Motel*, the third part of Jean-Claude Van Itallie's *America Hurrah*. According to Van Itallie, he also wanted to set the whole of *America Hurrah* 'in a yellow submarine – I guess from the Beatles' song' (Shyer, 1989: 292), an idea certainly in tune with the 1960s celebration of 'getting stoned' alluded to by the song. He also revamped for show at Pratt Institute two dances that he had created for a Youth Theatre programme in Waco.

In the meantime, he earned his living as a special instructor for the Department of Welfare teaching brain-damaged children, some of pre-school age, whose motor skills he aroused with endless patience by simple means – hold chalk to paper and, slowly, slowly, eventually draw a line, splash paint over newspaper-covered floors and walls, crawl inch by inch – all of it, to Wilson's mind, an application of what he had learned from Byrd Hoffman. Some of the adult crawling on all fours in later productions, among them *Doctor Faustus Lights the Lights* (1992, text by Gertrude Stein), might well be memory traces of his hours of crawling about with children, thus extending his life experience into his art practice.

While he was still at Pratt, Wilson first met the dancer and choreographer Jerome Robbins, who invited him to offer a series of therapeutic exercises at his experimental centre, the American Theater Laboratory. Wilson recalled in 1999 that Robbins was curious about the way he worked with brain-damaged children while he, Wilson, 'had no idea' that he 'would ever work in the theatre and wasn't particularly interested in theatre' (quoted in Lawrence, 2002: 364). Wilson continues:

> I was studying architecture, but what I was doing was a sort of crossover between architecture and performance, design, and it was a time in the sixties where you had this crossover. Someone like [Robert] Rauschenberg would paint a goat and put it in the middle of the room, so it was painting or was it sculpture, sort of coming off the wall and becoming three dimensional? And some of the work I was doing with children was free work, and I guess really related to theatre.
>
> (Ibid.)

Wilson's reference is to Rauschenberg's *Monogram* (1955–59), a painted goat poking its head and body through the hole of a tyre. Provocative in the avant-garde mode of the time, *Monogram* may well have had no allegorical or symbolic intention, although art historian Robert Hughes claims it is one of the wittiest statements ever to be made on sexual penetration (Pegram, 1980) and is 'one of the few great icons of male homosexual love in modern culture' (Hughes, 1991: 335). Wilson, it is clear, was attracted by the work's non-determined (*not* 'indeterminate') status, this being integral to the creative endeavour of the 1960s that sustained his unique approach. It will become evident in the course of this book how the kid of the 1960s survived in the international man of the twenty-first century.

When Wilson returned to New York after constructing *Poles*, he came back to the two areas in which he had been most active: teaching-enabling *through* performance and working *on* performance. The former included his activities with the terminally ill at Goldwater Hospital on Welfare Island where he organised a performance with patients in wheelchairs. Another was with patients in iron lungs who, by means of a system of dangling strings and pulleys devised by Wilson, moved fluorescent streamers and rolled-down posters with their mouths. His work *on* performance mostly took place in his Spring Street loft. Wilson made four pieces between 1967 and 1969. The first, *Baby*, was composed of disconnected sequences which featured rings and candles moved by hooded figures, and Wilson 'walking like an equilibrist on a narrow wooden plank using a giant lollipop as equilibrating stick' (Libe Bayrak in Brecht, 1994: 31).

The second, *Theatre Activity 1*, featured dancer Kenneth King, another early influence, and Andy de Groat, the choreographer for Wilson's path-breaking *Einstein on the Beach* in 1976. Some of the performers sat in the audience with their heads covered by paper bags. At one point, the performers on the stage blew bubbles, but nothing else happened. At another, the movements of a soldier-like figure, crashing glass and a soundtrack in the background appeared to be 'all about Vietnam' (Fanny Brooks in Brecht, 1994: 36). If true, then it suggests that, for all his immersion in the world of the imagination, Wilson was not oblivious to the violent antagonisms in the United Sates over the Vietnam War. The bag-covered heads were possibly a metaphor for the people blinkered by the War, although just how much semantic content was invested in the show's images is a matter of conjecture. Whether Wilson's works actually have semantic content and meaning or are purely 'aesthetic' constructions has remained a problematical issue ever since.

The next piece, *Theatre Activity 2*, took up the motif of crashing glass. The fourth, *ByrdwoMAN*, included Meredith Monk, a performer and innovator of music theatre. Composed, like its predecessors, of numerous disjointed bits, some static, others busy, *ByrdwoMAN* was in two parts, and lasted about two hours. Wilson played the role of the Byrdwoman in the first part in his loft, its floor covered with hay. A parrot in a cage, perhaps a joke on the 'character', sat at the back of the loft. Monk played the role in the second part in nearby Jones Alley, to which the audience was transported by two trucks. She danced in the street while somebody else descended a fire escape and Byrdwoman figures dotted nearby rooftops. Lawrence Shyer records: 'The audience was then taken around to the other side of the alley where they found nearly 40 Byrdwoman figures bouncing on wooden boards. At the conclusion of the performance, a rock band played and performers and spectators danced together' (Shyer, 1989: 293). Wilson performed with Monk again in 1968 in his duet *Alley Cats* for her piece *Co-op*. His contribution included performers bouncing up and down in long fur coats, which Monk found 'witty and fun' (ibid.: 296) – Wilsonian traits, although not usually associated with him.

The little information available about these performances manages to suggest the effervescence of the 1960s: wild imagination, naïve hedonism, tomfoolery, narcissism posing as artistic experimentation and serious innovation looking like narcissism. Wilson's loft-generated performances were, in effect, more like 'Events' (the first in 1964), as understood by Merce Cunningham and his partner John Cage, both of whom had made a lasting impact on Wilson. They were even more like the visual-art 'Happenings' invented by Allan Kaprow virtually a decade earlier. Like 'Happenings', they looked casual and used found spaces rather than dedicated ones, theatres or galleries. Their playing around with the boundaries between spectators and participants – dissolved in the party concluding *ByrdwoMAN* – was a nod to a practice popularised in the late 1960s, notably by Julian Beck and Judith Malina of the Living Theatre, and Richard Schechner whose 'environmental' theatre abandoned the proscenium arch and mixed and mingled performers and spectators in a common space.

In 1968, Wilson named the team gathered around him the Byrd Hoffman School of Byrds in honour of his old teacher. Wilson even called himself 'Byrd', appropriating his mentor's identity while playing with ideas of gender in cross-dress appearances in his 'Happenings'.

The School of Byrds was a communal but fluid group providing him with hundreds of largely amateur performers for nearly a decade, some quite literally culled by Wilson from the streets. In 1968, as well, Wilson became the artistic director of the Byrd Hoffman Foundation, Inc. and began preparations for *The King of Spain*. It was performed at the Anderson Theatre in 1969, the first of his early works on a proscenium stage. This production, his change of status and the constitution of the Foundation ('legalised' when Wilson filed a Certificate of Incorporation for it in 1970) might be said to have kicked-off his professional career.

DANCE PLAYS, SILENT OPERAS AND WORDS

The King of Spain was essentially a preamble to *The Life and Times of Sigmund Freud* (1969) at the Brooklyn Academy of Music, Wilson's second proscenium theatre. Subtitled 'a dance play in three acts', it was performed in silence or, intermittently, to a muted sound score. *Freud* repeated several key images from *The King of Spain* – a man running continually at the back of the stage, cat legs the height of the stage striding across it, the back of the gigantic head of a figure in an arm chair – and added many more that were just as incongruous: a beach with real sand covering the vast stage; a black woman in a black Victorian dress to whose wrist was attached a large stuffed raven; a man with a snake; a cave around which were grouped lions, tigers, cows and sheep, among other animals that appeared to wander randomly in and out of the show; young half-naked men and women exercising beyond the cave. Freud walked with his wife or grandson, or sat at the mouth of the cave, among the beasts.

The character was played by a man whom Wilson had noticed, struck by his resemblance to Freud, at a New York station and had persuaded to perform in his production. When he could not for the last two of four performances, he was replaced by Jerome Robbins, whose high forehead and balding head could pass for those of Freud. Wilson added to his team of Byrds some 30 ordinary people recruited or, like Freud, found by chance, who walked on and off the stage, performing no one else but themselves. The play's links to Freud were tenuous, its interest lying, apart from its disconcerting images, in its open space, slow pace and unhurried duration, the whole lasting some four hours without a break. A chair took these hours to descend from the flies to Freud's table, drawing space and the passage of time. A similar demarcation of time–space was to be had from the performers crawling over the sand, or from the turtle pulled on a string infinitesimally slowly across the stage. Richard Foreman, founder of the Ontological-Hysteric Theatre in 1968, called the production 'one of the major stage works of the decade', explaining that Wilson's was a 'non-manipulative aesthetic' quite different from that of the theatre and comparable only to the 'one current among advanced painters, musicians, dancers and film-makers' which liberated spectators to discover the 'discoveries' of the artists by themselves (*Village Voice*, 1 January 1970).

Everything that had brought *Freud* into the illogical logic of dreams and the unconscious – *there* was the 'hidden' link to Freud – was realised again in *Deafman Glance* (1970). A flock of pink flamingos unexpectedly flew by in the 'sky'. A man-sized frog in a dinner jacket and bow tie sat poised for hours beside a dinner table before it jumped on to it and then sat down to sip a martini. An alligator repeatedly closed its mouth around the ankle of a woman. *Deafman Glance* multiplied its effects – and length – when Wilson added *Freud* to it for the 1971 Nancy Festival, which was followed by performances in Paris, his first engagements outside the United States (Figure 1.1). The Nancy Festival, which promoted

Figure 1.1 *Deafman Glance* (1971). Photograph by R. Nusimovici

exciting international theatre, was the initiative of the young lawyer Jack Lang, who, before and after he became French President François Mitterrand's Minister of Culture in 1981, helped to further Wilson's career not only in France, but in the rest of Europe.

Nancy buzzed while Paris, the citadel of high art, fell, spellbound by the 'miracle' of silence, as Louis Aragon, the French surrealist novelist, described *Deafman Glance* (Aragon, 1971: 3). In his famous letter to his dead friend André Breton, author of the 1924 *Surrealist Manifesto*, Aragon wrote:

> I have never seen anything more beautiful since I was born. Never has any spectacle ever got anywhere near this one because it is, at the same time, waking life and life with your eyes closed, the world of every day indistinguishable from the world of every night, reality mixed with dreams, everything that is inexplicable in the gaze of a deaf man.... Bob Wilson...is what we, from whom surrealism was born, dreamed would come after us and go beyond us.... Bob Wilson is a surrealist by his silence, although this can be said about all painters, but Wilson binds gesture and silence, movement and what cannot be heard.
>
> (Ibid.)

Such silence, Aragon argued, was virtually unidentifiable. The work's 60 performers had 'no other word but movement', but it was 'neither a ballet nor a piece of mime or an opera'. If anything, it was a 'silent opera' and an 'extraordinary freedom-producing machine' that critiqued 'everything we are used to' and liberated people's 'mind and soul' (ibid.: 15). Aragon's belief that the liberation of the psyche was essential for changing the world echoed an old surrealist precept, which, its origins forgotten, had become a rallying call for social revolution on both sides of the Atlantic during the upheavals of 1968. Other French critics followed Aragon's lead in calling *Deafman* an opera. Together, they must have inspired Wilson who, from here on, called all his works 'opera' and justified his choice of term by pointing out that 'opera comes from the Latin root for "works" and that's what he makes, "works for the theatre"' (Shyer, 1989: xx).

Wilson created another compendium out of his existing pieces in his 12-hour *The Life and Times of Joseph Stalin* in 1973. Billed by Wilson as an 'opera', *Stalin* combined most of *Freud* with parts of *Deafman Glance, Overture for a Deafman* (1971), which was something of a synopsis of the former, and sections from the 24-hour stage-adapted version of *KA MOUNTAIN AND GUARDenia TERRACE*, which Wilson and the Byrds had devised for the Shiraz Festival in Iran in 1972. The Shiraz production required a cast of about a hundred. In later years, Wilson's practice of recycling material took the more limited form of recall of visual, aural and kinetic images. The sound of shattering glass, for instance, noted earlier, returns persistently in productions as diverse as *Death Destruction and Detroit II* (1987), *Orlando* (1989), *Alice* (1992) and *Three Sisters* (2001), to name but a few.

Stalin may not have been short, but *KA MOUNTAIN*, running for seven days and seven nights, epitomised Wilson's love of the long haul. It was a site-specific fantasia, a ritual and a pilgrimage across the seven hills of the arid rocky terrain of the Haft Tan Mountain, and involved an old man's journey up one of these hills while a host of unconnected events occurred simultaneously on all seven. Every day a different Byrd played the old man as if to suggest, by the change of actor, the idea of the seven stages through which human life supposedly passes.

The old man paused at various stations identified by cut-outs of such symbols of Western civilisation as Noah's Ark, the Acropolis and the New York skyline (Figure 1.2). These served as relay points for the performers and were where the spectator-participants could stop and rest, if they had not dropped out already. (Indeed, few managed to last the week.) The winding path was strewn with cut-out replicas of the old man and of other human-size figures, cut-out pink flamingos, papier-mâché fish, apples and snakes, and real animals in cages. A dinosaur stood at the foot of the central mountain and another at its summit, where, on the seventh night, in a grand apocalyptic moment, the face of a seven-foot ape went up in flames. Several stations provided platforms for gibberish, when not for declamatory, ritualistic readings from the Bible, *Moby Dick* and other canonical texts. The mountain itself with its searing heat during the day and intense cold at night could be said to be the prime actor in this epic whose greatest significance probably lay in the personal inner journeys undergone by its makers.

Something about the silence of distance in *KA MOUNTAIN*, of events seen from afar but not heard, must have connected the whole experience in Wilson's mind to *Deafman Glance*. His muse during these several years was the young deaf–mute Raymond Andrews whom he had adopted and whose capacity to order the world in pictures had confirmed his belief that language was not indispensable for knowledge and communication.

Figure 1.2 *KA MOUNTAIN and GUARDenia TERRACE* (1972). Photograph by Bahman Djalali

Yet the sound of language, if not its meaning, continued to fascinate Wilson, and he increasingly drew inspiration from his second adopted child, Christopher Knowles, who joined the Byrds, aged 14, in time to write for and perform in *Stalin*. Knowles was slightly autistic, and his way of disassociating sounds, words and sentences from conventional sense and of making chains and variations out of them provided Wilson with a model for *A Letter for Queen Victoria*, which he wrote and directed in 1974. Knowles wrote additional texts for the production. Much of *Queen Victoria* was slyly comic, indicating how well aware Wilson and Knowles were of the language games they were playing.

Queen Victoria, probably Wilson's most exuberantly verbal piece, is full of random sentences, odd colloquialisms, grammatical errors, slipshod punctuation and play with syllables that change according to changes of a letter in them ('HAP', 'HATH', 'HAT') and are repeated again and again. It has non-sequitur monologues, and bits of dialogue, some of which are nonsensical, others like overheard conversation and still others like trivia pretending to be formal speech. Numbers replace characters. Thus:

1 THEY'VE HAD ICE MAKING MACHINES AROUND FOR A LONG TIME.
YOU CAN'T WIN THEM ALL MAN.
2 MANDY YOU JUST GOT MARRIED.
1 MANDY I GOT A GET A DIVORCE.
2 MANDY IT JUST NOT HUMAN.
...
1 THIS ACT WAS DELIBERATE AND PROVOKED
2 HE TOLD ME SOME DAY HE'D GET EVEN.

(Wilson, 1996: 57–8)

The cast included Wilson and Knowles, who performed strategically placed duos with gusto. Wilson's voice frequently rose in a crescendo, engaging Knowles in comedian-style repartee accompanied by vaudeville gestures. Designs by Knowles out of single letters, syllables or words were painted on backdrops, demonstrating his visual and spatial conception of language. Several patterns were read out aloud to juxtapose them against acoustic patterns and shapes. Numerous sounds – knocks, screams, gun shots, horse's hooves, a train shot, a whistle – punctuated speech, some of which was uttered by two or three speakers at once. All of it intended, as Gertrude Stein said of her plays, 'To tell what could be told if one did not tell anything' (Stein, 1970: x). Wilson's empathy with Stein has been greatly underestimated partly because her deconstruction of language is more adroit than his. Yet Wilson shares at a very profound level, beyond the attraction of verbal concoctions, her non-narrative, whimsical and reflexive aesthetic. This is precisely why he staged, with the affection reserved for mentors, her *Doctor Faustus* (cited earlier), *Four Saints in Three Acts* (1996, music by Virgil Thomson) and *Saints and Singing* (1998).

Queen Victoria incorporated a string quartet and two dancers whose continual dervish-like spinning was the legacy of Kenneth King, King having left the Byrds around the time of *Deafman Glance*. The different arts comprising the production – not as unity or synthesis, but as textured arrangement – established Wilson's trademark hybridity, which has also been described as 'total theatre', or *Gesamtkunstwerk* in the manner of Wagner (Marranca, 1996: 39; although the latter description is misleading because Wilson never sought, then or later, the *fusion* of elements central to Wagner's *Gesamtkunstwerk* project. What I have called 'textured arrangement' is a different proposition). By its use of music throughout the performance, *Queen Victoria* foreshadowed *Einstein on the Beach*, Wilson's first fully fledged piece of music theatre which was followed over the years, in a zigzag fashion – Wilson, never linear, branched out in several directions at once – by a wide range of productions that were music theatre in some sense of the word. Given *Einstein*'s important place in Wilson's body of work and, indeed, in twentieth-century performance history, the production will be the focus of my third chapter.

Queen Victoria was also the hub of a series of verbal pieces for two written and performed by Wilson and Knowles. All were titled *Dia Log*, each with a different subtitle (1974, 1975, 1976, 1977), the last of which was *Curious George* in 1980. After this date, he rarely collaborated with Wilson again. *The Wind*, a reading with Wilson, took place in 1998, and he wrote passages for *Death Destruction and Detroit III* (1999). Their friendship, however, has endured, and Knowles has successfully pursued an independent career as a visual artist, showing drawings at the International Art Fair in New York in 2005 that echoed his stage experience with Wilson.

Queen Victoria was the beginning of the end of the Byrds as a collaborative group. The burden of sustaining a large creative community had become too great and, by the time of *Einstein*, Wilson knew that he wanted to operate in a more professional context. Sheryl Sutton, who had been key to *Deafman Glance*, worked with him on *Einstein*, as did Andy de Groat. The new major contributors to the production were composer Philip Glass and dancer and choreographer Lucinda Childs. Wilson's decision was doubtless also motivated by the strong response to *Deafman* in France, which the couturier Pierre Cardin had brought to the theatre he owned in Paris from Italy, where Wilson and the Byrds were stuck, penniless and without a return ticket home. Its success, followed by that of *Overture for a Deafman* (also produced by Cardin) and of the staged version of *KA MOUNTAIN* in 1972 (after the Shiraz event) led to sponsorship of *Einstein* by the French Ministry of Culture headed by Michel Guy, a staunch supporter since *Deafman*. This official seal of approval and faith in him would have exerted some pressure on Wilson to give priority to professional standards over amateur enthusiasm. Pressure may have come, in addition, from the feeling that he owed his best to the loyal audiences that he had by now acquired. In 2006, 30 years after *Einstein*'s premiere in France, Wilson's followers there have been exposed to tens of his productions and exhibitions. They have become a Wilson public, comfortable with his idiom.

Wilson was to build a more devoted audience still in Germany where his work continues to be commissioned and received. His influence spiralled outwards from Germany across Europe, where various countries have financed him, one after another, holding him to the Continent even as he flies elsewhere – to Japan, Indonesia, Australia and, occasionally back home, where selected productions of his are imported ready-made from abroad. Very few in the past decades have actually been initiated, crafted or financed in the United States: ironically, this richest of countries could never come up with the funds for his expensive creations, and those that have travelled there from their European cradle have not necessarily been Wilson's finest. Nor have they been able to convey to North Americans the full range and variety of his work, or to develop audiences on the scale and consistency of his audiences in Europe. Simply, not enough people in the United States have seen enough of his work. All this has made Wilson an American–European director.

ART AND POLITICS: THE 1960s AND AFTER

Practical circumstances have determined Wilson's path, but the United States and, specifically, the culture of New York have nurtured him. The 'Events' consolidated over the years by Cunningham and Cage (Cunningham was still presenting them in 2005) had grown out of the famous *Theatre Piece 1* staged by Cage at Black Mountain College in 1952. It was a multi-focus affair of simultaneous, unrelated activities outside and in the aisles of concentric circles arranged so that spectators only saw parts according to where they were sitting (Harris, 1987: 226). Cage's piece, although original – it included four all-white paintings by Rauschenberg hanging from the rafters – was 'not conceived in a creative vacuum' (ibid.: 227). It was fuelled by the neo-dadaist movement in New York spearheaded by Marcel Duchamp, Cage's discovery of Artaud's *The Theatre and its Double* and its argument that the theatre was a visceral, *physical* rather then literary experience, Cage's involvement with French new music (Pierre Boulez, Pierre Schaeffer) and, through Cunningham, with American new dance, and his obsession with Zen Buddhism and the chance operations of the *I Ching*. He composed his music by consulting the *I Ching* to throws of a dice, thereby disproving the reigning assumption that art necessarily depends on its maker's intentions. The appeal of Cage's principle of controlled randomness, which Cage never abandoned, is evident in all the Wilson productions discussed so far.

Black Mountain was a hotbed of experimentation, running summer schools where its teachers, many of whom had fled Nazi persecution, encountered a younger generation of non-conformist artists grouped, like Cage and Rauschenberg, in the large cities. These teachers had been formed by the European modernism of the first three decades of the twentieth century – Expressionism, Dada, Constructivism, Surrealism, the Bauhaus – and contributed to the spread of its ideas and sensibilities across the coteries and studios of art and dance, notably in New York. Several of them had been in contact with the teachings of Wassily Kandinsky at the Bauhaus in Germany on the way colour stimulated the senses and the emotions.

Kandinsky reconnoitred a terrain explored by the nineteenth-century German poet Goethe and the Russian constructivist painter Kasimir Malevich, whom Kandinsky had known when he lived in Russia. But the networks of modernism reached into unexpected quarters. The spiritual dimension of colour, as conceived by Kandinsky, connected him to Rudolf Steiner, founder, at the beginning of the twentieth century, of Anthroposophy, which linked humans and nature to the world of the spirit. Steiner's own theory of colour both reflected and contributed to the prevailing modernist ethos which was transplanted to Black Mountain College as a filigree of contacts and affinities. It was difficult to see, in this filigree, who or what was the presiding influence, or whether, in the younger, American-born generation of Cage and Rauschenberg, the transmutations had produced something else again.

We could put it this way. Bauhaus non-contentual, 'abstract' relationships between space, shape and colour were in the same network of thought and execution as those explored by Malevich. It is this 'whole', which includes Malevich's all-black as well as all-white paintings, that prefigured Rauschenberg's canvases. The same 'whole' transmuted in the 1960s, but touched Wilson vitally through his contact with the art world. We shall note in Chapter 2 how Wilson's perception of colour as capable of stimulating emotion is tied in with the modernist currents from Europe that had been absorbed in the United States. The painters Barnett Newnam and Donald Judd, who, increasingly in the 1960s, emphasised the relationship between colour and volume, were part of this process. Both, to this day, are touchstones for Wilson, particularly Newnam's glowing rods and expanses of colour for which Wilson has found the equivalent, with light, for the stage.

Influences were also passed on directly – the case of illustrious Bauhaus émigrés, architect Walter Gropius and his painter colleague Laszlo Moholy-Nagy, also an explorer of shape and colour. Or they were filtered, at one remove, through art schools such as Pratt Institute where Wilson was blown away by the stream-of-consciousness lectures on the history of architecture given by Sybil Moholy-Nagy. Wilson was to acknowledge that Sybil Moholy-Nagy's non-coercive attitude had affected his working method (Grillet and Wilson, 1992: 11; Morey and Pardo, 2003: 13), while the array of disparate illustrations that she showed as she talked taught him that word and image need not coincide.

The immigrant culture was a force to be reckoned with in the making of American culture and it provided for the visual and plastic artists of the 1960s and 1970s the axiom that a work of art did not have to be about anything other than itself: its constituent components and how they were done were its subject and justification. Jasper Johns, who was close to Rauschenberg and painted backdrops for Cunningham's dances, 'said' as much in his canvases when he showed that they meant nothing more than met the eye: a painting of the American flag was just that and nothing else except the application of paint. The choreographer George Balanchine, whose sense of spaciousness and purity of line struck a deep chord in Wilson, affirmed that his ballets did not have to tell a story because they were about the 'logic of movement'. He was not

> trying to prove something quite other than the fact of dancing. I only wish to prove the dance by dancing. I want to say: 'If you should happen to like it, here they are: dancers dancing. They dance for the pleasure of it, because they wish to'.
>
> (Kirstein, 1984: 32)

Dedication to that which *is* rather than means was concentrated in the 'Minimalism' that emerged during this period, a movement identified by its belief in interdisciplinary strategies for transforming art; similarly, by its rejection of expressiveness as the motor force of art practice. Thus choreographers who, like Lucinda Childs, were associated with the Judson Dance Theatre sought collaborators beyond the precincts of dance, and found them among painters and sculptors.

All, whatever, their 'originating' discipline backed Minimalism's ideology of non-expressive 'cool' and its tenet that art works were not the fulfilment of personality but, in the words of Johns, 'objects alone' (Francis, 1984: 50).

Once object status was conferred upon a performing form like dance, it necessitated a corresponding impersonality in how dancers danced. Impersonality, which had always been a feature of Cunningham's choreography, marked Wilson's work from the beginning and has permeated everything he has done ever since. But it was embodied ingeniously in former Judson dancer Trisha Brown's *Roof Piece* (1973), a remarkable exercise in minimalist-style repetition by 14 dancers on a mile of rooftops in Manhattan. An object set-up by alienated dancers, it wittily subverted itself as such by being literally lifted out of the consumerist arena – gallery, theatre – on to a space where it could be seen by a few, and bought by none. Gratuitous by nature, it corresponded with Balanchine's creed of dancing 'for the pleasure of it'. Wilson's 40 Byrdwomen on roofs four years earlier was in a similar spirit.

Given the trends of these years, it is not surprising that Susan Sontag's 1961 essay, 'Against Interpretation', should have had such great resonance for contemporary artists, including, of course, Wilson who was to collaborate with her in the 1990s. Nothing could have legitimated their practice more than her proclamation: 'Interpretation, based on the highly dubious theory that a work of art is composed of items of content, violates art. It makes art into an article of use, of arrangement into a mental scheme of categories' (Sontag, 1994: 10). And the value that she ascribed, against content, to the 'sensuous surface' and the 'sensory experience of the work of art' (ibid.: 13) valorised their experiments with form for the gratification of the senses. The most humorous example was Cage's incorporation of everyday, ready-made sounds in his *4′33″*. A pianist sat at a keyboard in silence while the noises of the street filled the room, obliging the audience to listen, instead of blocking them off, and then to hear them as the composition itself. The event demonstrated Cage's contention in *Silence*, allegedly 'the one book' Wilson, 'a non-reader', cites as 'having had an important effect on his thinking' (Stearns, 1984: 64), that there was no such thing as silence at all. There were always ambient sounds, including your heartbeat, which are 'only called silence because they do not form part of a musical intention' (Cage, 1987: 22).

Looking back, it would seem that Wilson's silent pieces were influenced by Cage, and he shared Cage's interest in how the always-there was changed by changed perception; similarly, in how perception could embrace multiple foci and yet shift attention by choice. Cunningham developed this idea in his dance: all points were equally the 'centre' of the dance and there were no fixed points in space (Cunningham, 1991: 18). As a consequence, the onus for what they saw was on spectators. Wilson's decentred, mosaic pieces transferred responsibility in the same way. Childs said as much of the two-hander made up of roughly a hundred story fragments that she and Wilson co-directed and performed in 1977, *I Was Sitting on my Patio This Guy Appeared I Thought I was Hallucinating* (text by Wilson). It was the spectator's job, she asserted, 'to make sense of what he sees and to decide if it's chaos or order, formed or formless, or if that matters' (quoted in Shank, 2002: 134).

'COOL' AND 'HOT'

Wilson's taste for the culture of cool was behind his dismissal of the radical, hot arts epitomised by the Living Theatre who had arrived with a bang in 1959 with their production of Jack Gelber's *The Connection*. The company, led vociferously by Beck and Malina (although leadership contradicted its anarchist politics), had defied social mores and state authorities, including the Inland Revenue Service which seized their theatre in 1963. It went into voluntary exile in Europe, spreading the cause of revolution in the streets as much as in the theatre. For, Beck claimed again and again, there was no distinction between theatre and life, and what counted even more than theatre-as-life was action.

The Living Theatre was particularly aggressive in France in 1968 during the insurrections of May, inciting students to occupy the state-owned Odéon Theatre in Paris. Then, with an extreme-left group calling itself the *enragés*, it sabotaged the state-endowed Avignon Festival where it was to perform *Paradise Now*. Denouncing the Festival, with the *enragés*, as an instrument of bourgeois oppression, it refused to honour its engagement and returned to the United States, publicity for its exploits preceding it, to perform in that symbolic year of 1968 that no less symbolic *Paradise Now*. The production, with its agit-prop political messages, group groping of naked bodies on stage and assumed intimacy with spectators – the actors came down off the boards to caress, animate, accost and harangue them – appeared to crystallise not just the ideal of individualism, which was part of the national ethos, or a flagrantly hedonistic idea of unfettered freedom, which was not so familiar, but the deeply political as well as life-style concerns, the whole gamut of the so-called counter-cultural concerns, of a whole decade.

Why was this so? The answers are far from simple and the requisite historical information has been well documented (Caute, 1988; Heale, 2001; Jones, 1995; Wilmeth and Bigsby, 2002). The roots of the counter-culture's questioning of received values went deep into the 1950s – the destabilisation of liberalism and the American Dream by McCarthyism and its anti-communist witch-hunts, and the fear of the atom bomb, fed by the Cold War. Wilson, who was growing up in these years, could not help but be exposed to these national traumas, even in a small place like Waco. And he remembers the 'absurd' public instruction, when he was a child, to hide for protection under a table in the event of a bomb being dropped (9 February 2005, during a rehearsal of *Peer Gynt*). Doubts about materialism, consumerism and other givens of the American way of life led, in some quarters, to sullen anger and, in others, to cultivated insouciance. Allen Ginsberg, poet of the Beat Generation, conveyed this anger. Novelist William Burroughs's tone was very much on the wry side – the 1950s version of 'cool' – and his promotion of drug-induced alternatives to conventional society (notoriously in *The Naked Lunch*, 1959) made him a precursor of the 1960s hippies. He was to have a new lease of life when Wilson sought him out for collaboration on the text of *The Black Rider* (1990).

All this questioning fed Malina and Beck's view that the Living Theatre should contest the status quo. But it had a much wider reach. It developed the critical awareness that flared up in the 1960s and 1970s which, Maldwyn Jones writes, 'were among the most traumatic decades in American history':

> The country was shaken by a sequence of political assassinations and by a protracted, shabby and shaming scandal. A new and aggressive militancy among blacks and other disconnected groups produced violent confrontations on the street and college campuses. A costly, frustrating and ultimately unsuccessful war plunged the nation into turmoil, while shattering the 'illusion of American omnipotence'. These experiences left Americans divided and unsure of themselves. Some carried their rebelliousness to the point of questioning the very moral and constitutional foundations of American society. Meanwhile America's economic supremacy was being

> eroded: there was mounting worry about inflation, unemployment, and the
> threat of an energy shortage. National pride did indeed receive a boost in
> 1969 from the remarkable technological achievement of landing a man on
> the moon and from the bicentennial celebrations of 1976. But the late 1970s
> brought a further darkening of the economic skies as well as more humili-
> ating reminders of the limits of American power.
>
> (Jones, 1995: 543)

Most notable among the assassinations were those of President John
F. Kennedy in 1963 and the black civil rights leader Martin Luther King
in 1968:

> within minutes of the news being broadcast [of King's assassination by a
> white] African Americans were taking to the streets. Riots broke out in
> over a hundred cities, and within a week forty-six people died and 27, 000
> were arrested. Over 700 fires lit up Washington D. C.
>
> (Heale, 2001: 123)

Such riots demonstrated the magnitude of a problem where poverty,
race, discrimination and exclusion were tightly intermeshed. These
were issues fiercely attacked by Black Power groups (a concept King did
not approve) like the Black Panthers and the separatist Black Muslims
who, whatever they may have ultimately gained for their communities,
were instrumental in focusing attention on the principles of citizenship –
rights, entitlements, obligations and respect for identities – integral to
any democracy. Their example stirred the consciousness of white people
and emboldened Mexican Americans, Asian Americans and Native
Americans to stake out their own claims not solely to ethnic identity,
but also to political equality.

The theatre contributed to this process. An impressive list of black
playwrights included Lorraine Hansberry, from an earlier generation,
and Amiri Baraka, from the more recent Black Muslim radicals, who
had changed his name from LeRoi Jones. El Teatro Campesino made
interventionist performances in collaboration with Chicano farm workers. By the late 1970s, it had become less militant on the grounds that
conditions for Chicano farm workers had improved and the company
now had to look to its artistic growth. The San Francisco Mime Troupe,
wholly engaged in the politics of empowerment, performed among the
Italian, Asian and Chicano communities. Founded in 1959, it was 'one

of the oldest of the contemporary theatres dedicated to bringing about social change' (Shank, 2002: 59) and one of the most consciously dedicated to the working classes. By the end of the 1970s, it was still committed to its leftist platform in the *commedia dell'arte*, circus and carnival side-show style that it had made its own.

Pressure groups for civil rights involved, beside ethnic 'minorities', gay, women's and feminist groups of various kinds, all more or less galvanised by the Vietnam War. Probably the War alone could bring about some agreement across the gender divide between the men burning draft cards and the women burning bras, or the race divide, since it had become clear to all that combat troops were disproportionately composed of African Americans, or the divide between students and parents, who disapproved of their offspring's cavalier attitude to sex. Peace protests were a uniting force, evident particularly in the massive march concluding Stop the Draft Week in October 1967 on the Pentagon.

Marches, sit-ins and demonstrations, many of them violent, continued when the War was extended to Cambodia, the Kent State University demonstration in 1970 being infamous for the shooting of four students by national guardsmen. Richard Nixon was now President, and his administration's ruthless drive against civil disobedience, supported by what had become known as the 'silent majority', heralded a right-wing backlash as anti-liberal as it was anti-left. Conservatism took hold on all fronts, surviving the Watergate scandal (concerning eavesdropping devices placed by Nixon's men in the Democratic Party's headquarters), which brought about the impeachment of Nixon and the downfall of his presidency in 1974. It survived, as well, the more benign but weak presidency of Jimmy Carter, who was elected in 1976, the year of *Einstein*.

However, conservatism took off virulently in the Ronald Reagan 1980s whose agendas for traditional social values (many, like anti-abortion campaigns, renouncing the rights won by women two decades earlier) began to stifle protest and whose political programmes, especially on the international scene, aimed to reinvent American supremacy. The Reagan period returned to Cold War tactics (the Soviet Union was 'the Evil Empire'), bequeathing to George Bush, who was elected in 1988, the bellicose turn of mind and greed for oil that gave the Gulf War (1992) and later, under the leadership of the latter's son, the Iraq War (2003). Reaganite economic policies, on the other hand, held to neo-liberal, aggressively competitive *laissez-faire* principles, which have continued to the present day, shifting gear according to the pressures of the market and the corporations regulating them. Reagan's legacy in social life took the form of quietism, defined at the turn of the twenty-first century as 'political correctness'.

FINANCE AND FORMALISM

A huge amount of history has necessarily been elided, my signposts intended to provide a rough context for Wilson in and beyond his formative years. I have stressed his formative years because they situate *Einstein on the Beach* – also by what *Einstein* is *not* – which is an exceptional work, even for this period of contention and invention, and seminal to Wilson's artistic development and his international career. Furthermore, although Wilson was extraordinarily productive in the decades that followed, superseding some of his achievements in *Einstein*, as in other works, *Einstein* was to remain a reference not only for the theatre (dance and opera included) and the visual arts, but also for those arts transgressing boundaries to become new, hybrid genres.

The radicalism, in all senses of the term for the 1960s and 1970s, met with the opposition that pushed towards the turn to the right initiated by Nixon. And the right was allergic to the very idea of government intervention in the economic sphere, which also transferred to the arts. Thus, one of Reagan's first decisions when he came to power was to cut the funds of the National Endowment for the Arts, a recent body, since it was founded only in 1965. Wilson was well aware of the implications of Reagan's action, observing in an interview at the time that 'Reagan and his men spend money on bombs and arms. This is a disgrace for our country, for art in our country' (Friedl, 1982: 58). And he compared it to the very different relationship between government and the arts in France and Germany (ibid.). At this point in his career, the beginning of the 1980s, France and Germany were his foremost patrons.

Indeed, comparison with Europe on the role of the state in civil society is illuminating. The *principle* of state subsidy for the arts does not depend, in Europe, on the position of a government on the left or the right of the political spectrum. A state cultural policy is in place irrespective of who is in power and how its programme may shift. What changes is the degree of subsidisation. This is precisely why Wilson's work was able to enjoy the support of the French state in the early and mid-1970s, when the government was on the right of the spectrum under Presidents Pompidou and Giscard d'Estaing, and continued to enjoy it during the 1980s, when the government was on the left and Mitterrand in power.

Support in the 1980s was greater still from the Federal Republic of Germany, first, because the country had the highest national budget for the arts in Western Europe and, second, because its two-tiered subsidy system provided funds from both the Federal government and wealthy municipal councils. Overall funding decreased after the unification of Germany (1990), but such theatres as the Schaubühne am Lehniner Platz in Berlin, which had commissioned work from Wilson previously, continued to house his shows when they were not able to produce them. The rest of Western Europe ascribes to cultural policies that guarantee subsidies to theatres. Wilson's work was able to benefit from them in the 1990s (Italy, Spain) and after 2000 (Denmark, Sweden, Norway) while retaining favour in France and Germany, the two countries that had launched him.

Of course, the Unites States had the National Endowment for the Arts. However, it was small fry, even before Reagan's cuts, when compared to state subsidies in Europe, and small compared to the private Foundations that are the veritable patrons of the arts in the United States. Wilson has been the recipient of such Foundations – the Rockefeller Foundation, the Guggenheim Fellowship – but his work in all its variety has required numerous permanent benefactors. The Watermill Centre, completed and inaugurated in 2006, is an international laboratory founded by Wilson in 1992 for interdisciplinary collaboration – research, preparation of new works and teaching. A massive, remarkable undertaking, it has relied heavily on the private patronage assured by Wilson's high international profile and the managerial and fund-raising skills of his administrative team. Wilson ploughs his earnings into Watermill whose operation in the future is bound to require considerable financial resources.

Institutions of state cannot run indefinitely without public backing, and the great response from the French public to *Deafman Glance* and *Einstein on the Beach*, which had toured nationally, suggested audiences had shed some of the anti-American sentiment that had flared up in France in the early 1960s. All the countries of Western Europe had had revolts in 1968 specific to their political, socio-economic and cultural conditions. But their left-wing and liberal groups shared their opposition to the Vietnam War, drawing strength from the anti-war movements in the United States. This meant a general change in attitude. Things were no longer dismissed as 'American', and such evidence of people power and free speech as the exposure of Watergate by the press, which helped to bring Nixon to justice, was taken as a model of democracy at work. By 1976, when *Einstein* was performed, these positive political images of the United States in France had merged with the perception that its arts were just as daring. The French political and artistic elites heavily promoted North American artists, especially their 'cool' variety — Wilson, Cunningham, Cage, Brown, Childs, Monk and Foreman. Meanwhile, the French state paid for their work.

But let us go back to Wilson in the United States. Wilson was reticent about 'hot' politics and this, together with his immersion in avant-garde dance, music, painting and design, but *not* the theatre, could be taken as a sign of his political attitude. Perhaps the best way of putting it is through Henry Sayre's observation that Brown's *Roof Piece* 'also represents, I think, the relative isolation of dance from the social, let alone political, arena'. Sayres continues:

> While avant-garde dance and music have both succeeded in providing important formal models for the avant-garde, they have remained, as it were, aesthetic. Few people know about either, and fewer are willing to read into their performances implicit political positions.
>
> (Sayre, 1989: 140)

And yet: 'Insofar as she [Brown] creates "objects" which cannot be contained in "consumer space," her work assumes a political dimension' (ibid.). The issue emerging from Sayre's discussion is trickier still when the 'objects' of such visual artists as Andy Warhol, whose 'scene' Wilson had frequented, enter the picture. Do Warhol's repeated ready-made images of American icons, whether Campbell's soup cans or Marilyn Monroe, have a political dimension in so far as they can be taken to be wry, 'cool' musings on objects in 'objects' and on the act of consumption itself? Perhaps, but does the fact that they *are* contained in 'consumer space', and made Warhol millions, deny them a political dimension?

Attitude is a simpler issue than dimension, and Warhol's stemmed from his dandyism. Dandy 'cool' rather than passion defined Wilson's take on the world. When it came to 'political dimension', he preferred it in the detached manner of Laurie Anderson, who wrote the music for his staging of *Alcestis* in 1986; and her performance hybrids were closer to his own than anything in the theatre, notwithstanding the experiments in form and genre of Mabou Mines and those generating the mixed popular-theatre forms of El Teatro Campesino and the Bread and Puppet Theatre. The Living Theatre was not attractive to Wilson, but nor were Joseph Chaikin's collectively run Open Theatre or Megan Terry's politicised productions (her extravagant anti-war *Viet Rock* in 1966 was a milestone in musicals). Nor was he inspired by the burgeoning gay or feminist theatres, among them the lesbian group Split Britches. And none had anything much in common with his work, although all had rejected the orthodoxies of story, plot and character construction, realistic acting and spectator identification with the stage, as Wilson himself had done.

Arnold Aronson describes Wilson's theatre as 'formalist', comparable, as such, virtually only to that of Richard Foreman (Aronson, 2000a: 140; also Shank, 2002: 12):

> the formalist theatre could be seen as a reversion to the American myth of the lone explorer forging new paths in the wilderness. With its rejection of the emotionally cathartic experience, formalist theatre could be seen as a response to the failure of alternative life styles to transform society in the significantly utopian ways that had been anticipated.
>
> (Ibid.: 146)

Elsewhere Aronson argues that Wilson and Foreman's theatre was

> the product of a unique and very personal vision. Although complex spiritual, social and political ideas entered into their works to varying degrees at different points throughout their careers, ideology was neither the starting point of the creative endeavour nor the goal of the performance, as it tended to be for the majority of 1960s experimental groups.
>
> (2000b: 111)

The trends of the 1960s ceded to the many different directions taken by the theatre of the 1980s and the 1990s, graphed admirably by Theodore Shank (2002). Wilson's work of these decades has points in common with the performance art of the period and, curiously, with Elizabeth LeCompte and the Wooster Group whose collaborative practice grew out of the 1960s, its methods possibly closer to the Open Theatre than anyone else.

The Wooster Group's work in the past 30 years might not be formalist in Aronson's sense of the term, but its concern with composition and with technology for formal purposes, and its highly complex social ideas, which elude classification as 'ideology', are by no means alien to the Wilson of today.

And what of Foreman? Foreman has followed his star to his allegedly last stage work ever in 2005, *THE GODS ARE POUNDING MY HEAD (AKA Lumberjack Messiah)*. Quirky, and humorous as only a 'broken heart' can be (Foreman's phrase in his programme note), it bids farewell to the lumberjacks of the avant-garde 'forging', in Aronson's words, 'new paths in the wilderness'. Wilson, meanwhile, continues to pursue his vision, but not as a lone explorer and certainly not in any wilderness, real or metaphorical.

WILSON AFTER *EINSTEIN*

Aronson's claim that Wilson's 'was a singular vision created through total control of the creative and producing processes' (2000a: 146) is relevant for his Byrd Hoffman beginnings, but does not apply categorically to his work with established artists and the staff of established theatres. Or, rather, what changes subtly with and after *Einstein on the Beach* is the collaborative model. The laid-back, communal style of the Byrds shifted to a collaboration among professional peers, and this more high-powered mode spawned variations, the strongest being what could be called Wilson's 'corporate' model, which he perfected as the 1990s moved into the twenty-first century.

The dizzying volume of Wilson's output and, after about 2000, its increasingly rapid flow make it impossible to itemise in the short space of this book. I shall, therefore, proceed by clusters, grouping productions by shared characteristics, as earlier for his silent pieces or his *Dia Log* 'series' with Knowles. This organisation is not chronological, although it is temporal, and it is not foolproof since some pieces in one cluster could well cross into another, as might be expected of work that by its very nature slips over borders. Not all of Wilson's theatre works will be cited, and his designs, exhibitions and related visual-art activities are here excluded.

DISLOCATED HISTORY

Wilson's productions of the early to mid-1980s have a distinctly historical bent. However, their 'social and political ideas', in Aronson's words, are not elaborated, nor embedded in issues and consequences, which is part of what we think of as history. They are allusions largely derived from anecdotes, and they give an impressionistic overview in which colour, light and shape suggest rather than tell what fills the canvas. This is primarily due to how an image rather than a verbal account triggers off Wilson's imagination, leading him to collate information in ways that are frequently enigmatic. Historical content, then, is never direct or straightforward. It is dislocated and deviated through pathways that meander through his productions, but only show where they may have been going when they are retraced, backwards, so to speak, after the event.

One of these pathways concerns 'great' individuals: Rudolf Hess, Adolf Hitler's Deputy Führer, in *Death Destruction and Detroit* (1979) and Thomas Edison, the American inventor of the incandescent electric lamp, in *Edison* (1979). The 'heroes' of *the CIVIL warS* (1983–85), an epic of grand proportions claiming to encompass nothing less than the history of the world, are Abraham Lincoln and Robert E. Lee, opponents in the American Civil War, Frederick the Great, eighteenth-century King of Prussia and military mogul, and Guiseppe Garibaldi, whose battles led to Italy's unification in 1861.

Death Destruction and Detroit was Wilson's first production for the Schaubühne in Berlin, known internationally for the radical organisational and artistic innovations of Peter Stein, its director from 1970. This production – Wilson's first experience of a strong ensemble company, even though he used only a few actors from it – provides clear examples of historical dislocation. A photograph of Hess as an 82-year old man staring into empty space in Spandau prison caught Wilson's attention and, although it had little to do with the sketches forming in his head, it slowly drew him to Hess's story, snatches of which began to encroach upon his material. The research of his co-writer Maita di Niscemi threw up details about Hess's solo flight to Scotland in 1941 (supposedly to obtain peace), his crash landing and, finally, his solitary confinement by the allies in Spandau. The alleged words of the Scottish farmer who had witnessed his landing, 'Come, let's have a cup of tea with my mum' (Shyer, 1989: 96), are uttered in a scene where a parachutist descends on a 'street' in London. They are out of context and very cryptic, in any case, in the scenic context. (How many spectators could possible guess the origin of these words?!)

Haphazard though they appear to be, they relate circuitously to other details such as the goggles worn in a totally different scene by women driving egg-shaped cars in a desert (Figure 1.3). The goggles are a replica of the ones worn by Hess, while the cars and the desert are part of a fictitious iconography unrelated to him. The unreal looking cars seem purely arbitrary until they are linked to a recurring phrase in another scene, 'You're from Detroit'. Detroit was once a major automobile manufacturing city, and Shyer maintains that the phrase relates the German war machine to the assembly-line production of American industry, where 'dreams of power and destruction are also generated' (Shyer, 1989: 99). The photograph of Hess raking leaves in Spandau prison's garden with two other inmates undergoes a metamorphosis in Wilson's image of three blind men tapping their way across the stage with their canes. The men's caps and costumes are similar to those worn by Hess. The canes allude to his increasing loss of sight in old age. History thus appears on the microstructure of personal detail rather than on the macrostructure of issues, but, even then, to be fully visible it needs to be reconstructed through Wilson's creative process.

Figure 1.3 *Death Destruction and Detroit* (1979). Photograph by Ruth Walz, courtesy of Ruth Walz

Reconstruction might be possible for researchers, but is impossible for spectators, so the point of the work is to allow them to connect at will from a phenomenal collage of material. Of course, Wilson's elliptical approach is not without its pitfalls, and *Death Destruction and Detroit* led to confusion among those German spectators who expected 'serious cultural and political critique' (Arens, 1991: 37) instead of the link that Wilson gave them of a 'political event to everyday life and objects' (ibid.). Whether you view this critically or with pleasure, the theme of war in *Death Destruction and Detroit* is so cunningly displaced that it seems not to be there at all.

The CIVIL warS provides an apposite contrast, although it also works on principles of ellipsis and allusion. Wilson's premise here is that war is a universal of all time, sweeping up all humanity, and is potently conveyed by film images projected onto a screen the height and breadth of the stage. Vast walls of buildings ceaselessly crash down, image after image, as if whole cities were repeatedly being detonated by bombs. The cumulative effect is awesome and no less so when a group of ordinary-looking people place themselves in front of the screen, one by one, while the continuing images of annihilation are projected over them. They smile and, suddenly, because of the motion behind them, they look like photographs of the dead turned up against the debris. This sequence is the closest Wilson has ever come to making a socio-political statement, and it possibly recollects the nuclear threat of his childhood and youth. *The CIVIL warS* could also be his belated response to the strife of the 1960s, as suggested by Wilson's claim that he thought of 'war' as civil conflict and struggle of every kind (Brookner, 1985).

The CIVIL warS was dislocated quite literally, Wilson having decided to break it up into sections to be built, rehearsed and performed in different cities – Rotterdam, Cologne, Minneapolis, Rome, Marseille and Tokyo, with workshops in Munich and Freiburg, among other locations. The whole, constituting five acts and a connecting Noh-like interlude (the Minneapolis section, 1984), was to be assembled in a 12-hour performance at the Olympic Arts Festival during the Los Angeles Olympics in 1984. As Shyer observes: 'With its theme of universal brotherhood, its diverse cultural make-up and international cast, *the CIVIL warS* was a mirror of the Olympics itself. The occasion of its presentation was really part of its form' (Shyer, 1985: 75). Wilson had indeed foreseen this correspondence, and had the climax come at the end of the Rome section, the fifth act, which recapitulates the motifs of the earlier sections. Thus Alcmene, who is the mother of Hercules, the founder of the Olympics, hands him the torch of peace. (Texts by Seneca are mixed with those of di Niscemi.) Luxurious pictures of the world's vegetation slide by on the scrim to recover the battlefields of the dead. Nature, beasts and humans are one. Hercules holds aloft the torch that opens the Olympics and promises a new future.

The Rotterdam (1983), Cologne (1984) and Rome sections (1984) had already been performed in their home cities and Wilson was in Tokyo making final preparations for that section when the Director of the Olympic Arts Festival announced the cancellation of *the CIVIL warS*: another $1.2 million, still needed, could not be found. This announcement occurred, without prior consultation with Wilson, three months before the scheduled premiere in Los Angeles. Wilson had already rejected a proposed compromise to show one or two section at the Olympics rather than the whole work. Wilson:

> I couldn't do it. I just couldn't. The Italians spent hundreds of thousands of dollars on their production. They painted those beautiful drops over a hundred meters long, it cost a hundred thousand dollars just for the drums that held them up. They built the show for Los Angeles as well their own tiny opera house in Rome, and then they flew everyone out to California to study the theatre. In Japan, schoolchildren and artists sent in contributions. The Germans spent so much on the production and the French... How could I say to them 'I'm only going to take this section?' These are the people who support my work. I couldn't do it. I couldn't choose one over another.
>
> (Shyer, 1985: 74)

Nor did Wilson give up without a fight. Having run out of money of his own, and in debt everywhere (he owed $45,000 on the scenery for the Japanese section alone), he came up with the ingenious idea of broadcasting the performance live by simultaneous satellite from the countries of all the sections. He secured the support of French and German radio and television, but to no avail. The work was cancelled, leaving a shattered Wilson to observe how difficult it was in America 'to find a sponsor for something that's unknown' (ibid.: 75) and to despair at his country's lack of subsidies for serious art. 'I'm always saying,' Wilson observes, 'that what we need is a national cultural policy' (ibid.). Los Angeles, home to Hollywood, seemed hardly the right place to try, and its commercial outlook was perfectly in harmony with the Reagan era.

Wilson spent five years on *the CIVIL warS*, working with hundreds of performers, writers, choreographers and composers who spoke different languages, and the multi-lingual aspects of its five acts reflect this international interchange. Among the throng was Glass, who wrote the music for the Rome section. A new collaborator Suzushi Hanayagi, who was to become a long-term one, choreographed the Minneapolis section. Wilson was to learn more about the stylisation of movement from her. Another new collaborator was Heiner Müller whom Wilson had invited to write the Cologne section. Müller tailored his texts to Wilson's visual needs, understanding full well his faith in the power of imagery since his own playwriting was viscerally imagistic, crammed full of jagged angles and incongruities, like Wilson's staging. His writing similarly ignored narrative and characterisation and, although tighter, tougher and more violent than Wilson's scenic as well as verbal writing, its grit provided a foil for the beauty of Wilson's productions. Müller, moreover, became an intellectual mentor, whose erudition and harsh experiences in Germany during the Second World War and afterwards in East Germany fed Wilson's untutored intelligence.

Müller was to give Wilson his fragmented play *Despoiled Shore Media Material Landscape with Argonauts* for the Prologue to the opera *Medea*, (1984, music by the English avant-garde composer Gavin Bryars), and *Description of a Picture* for the Prologue to *Alcestis* (music by Laurie Anderson, as noted previously; choreography by Hanayagi). *Alcestis* was American-made, among the few in Wilson's repertoire, and its presentation by the American Repertory Theatre (ART) in 1986 gave Wilson some cause for optimism after the fallout of *the CIVIL warS:* like all prophets, he wanted recognition in his own country.

Müller came to work with him on *Alcestis* at ART as well as on *Hamletmachine* in English with students at New York University, which he revised for Wilson's production. Wilson amplified Müller's short play to some three hours of performance, asserting thereby, to Müller's delight, the independence of *mise en scène* from text. When, in the same year, he directed *Hamletmaschine* with German actors from the Thalia Theatre in Hamburg – hereafter an important patron of his work – Wilson started a pattern that entailed revivals of the same production in another language. The second in this mode was an English version of Müller's *Quartett* (1988, presented again by ART), which doubled the German version of 1987. Müller subsequently contributed a text to *Death Destruction and Detroit II* (1987) for Berlin's Schaubühne and to

The Forest based on the Gilgamesh epic, which was commissioned by Berlin for its City of Europe festival (1988). His intense period of work with Müller provoked Wilson to confront, in Müller's words, the 'power of images with history and the European experience' (quoted in Shyer, 1989: 133), and left him with a different appreciation of language. He no longer saw language solely as sonic effect (the case of *A Letter for Queen Victoria*), but as a vehicle for *dramatic* structure. Müller was as much against interpretation as he was, so he continued to bypass language as a medium for semantic meaning.

ADAPTATIONS FROM PROSE

Wilson's re-experienced sense of the word through his collaboration with Müller showed in productions for which various writers adapted prose fiction for him. Largely solos and duos, they offered opportunities for rehearsal on a one to one basis with renowned European actors: Jutta Lampe of Schaubühne fame, French film star Isabelle Huppert, Denmark's Susse Wold and Britain's Miranda Richardson, all in the title role of *Orlando* after the novel by Virginia Woolf. *Orlando*, in German in 1989, was followed by the French and Danish versions in 1993 and the English version in 1996 at the Edinburgh Festival. Among the fine male actors whom he encountered was stage and screen star Michel Piccoli, a key player with Patrice Chéreau and Peter Brook. Piccoli performed *La Maladie de la mort* by Marguerite Duras with Lucinda Childs. *La Maladie* was premiered in German at the Schaübuhne in 1991. Its French version with Piccoli and Childs toured Europe in 1996 and 1997, including London for the Peacock Theatre's one-off French Season in 1997.

Wilson's repeats in changing languages was a symptom of the globalisation that, by the mid-1990s, had seriously permeated the theatre, operating through well-oiled international circuits and relying on co-productions between theatres, festivals, agencies and related organisations. The global network certainly favoured Wilson economically and in terms of publicity, but it also provided artistic benefits, giving him access to highly capable people whom he would not otherwise have met. The great actors excited his imagination with their versatility, and the rhythms and intonations peculiar to their native languages showed him how atmosphere, a dramatic tool, can be created through different languages differently. In Germany, he worked for the first time with dramaturgs, learning from their deconstruction, reconstruction and contextualisation of texts. He developed his already sharp ear for sound from contact with brilliant music-sound designers like the German Hans Peter Kuhn whose multi-level scores for *La Maladie, Orlando, Alice in Bed* (text by Susan Sontag) at the Schaubühne in 1993 and *Hamlet: a monologue* in 1995, utilised state-of-the art technology, pushing the frontiers of sound composition. Wilson kept pace with technological developments with whose help he continued to stretch his vocabulary of sound.

Other Wilson prose adaptations during the 1990s include *The Meek Girl* (1994) for four actors based on Dostoevsky's story, and *Wings on Rock* (1998) based on *The Little Prince* by Antoine de Saint-Exupéry. As a whole, his prose cluster shows quite clearly Wilson's turn to the European canon for his source material, and it foreshadowed his interest in the European dramatic canon, to which, hitherto, he had given only sporadic attention.

DRAMA CLASSICS

Wilson performed in *The Meek Girl* after an absence of some ten years from the stage, and, for this reason, the production can be seen as a bridge to *Hamlet*, the last work involving him as a performer. Being a monologue, *Hamlet* links up with *Orlando* and, further back in time, to Chekhov's one-act monodrama *Swan Song*, staged in Munich in 1989. By the same token, it belongs to Wilson's Shakespeare group, Wilson having directed a small-scale, monologue-like *King Lear* in German in Frankfurt (1991) whose title role was played by the acclaimed German actress Marianne Hoppe. His third Shakespeare production was *The Winter's Tale*, also in German, at the Berliner Ensemble in 2005. By contrast with the preceding two, *The Winter's Tale* was on a full scale, retaining most of Shakespeare's characters and following his plot and sub-plot through to their resolution.

Hamlet is very much Wilson's *Hamlet*, several degrees removed from Shakespeare's text for having been cut down to one and a half hours of play. He deletes Fortinbras and other characters related to the theme of war, and plays all the parts centrally related to Hamlet himself. Role switches are indicated by a change of space, movement and voice, and by a costume or object that Wilson occasionally holds up in front of him. All deletions allow Wilson to focus on Hamlet's long journey through his thoughts about his personal relations and his place in the world. In this respect, the production is a mediation on space and time – a perspective taken right from the start when Wilson reverses Shakespeare's order and begins with Hamlet's 'Had I but time' (Act V, scene ii). The production closes with this line as well, providing a suitable framing device for its philosophical reflections. It has strong cabaret, vaudeville and camp components, but is nothing less than deeply moving.

A visual frame complements the verbal frame, which is a charcoal pile of 'slabs' at the back of the stage. In the opening scene, Wilson lies sideways, with his back to the audience, while saying 'Had I but time' (Figure 1.4). Elsewhere, he lies sideways facing the audience, and this reversed image also shows that the 'slab' construction had diminished since the opening of the performance – a discreet allusion, perhaps, to the erosion of time by time. Suggesting weight, although elegantly arranged, these slabs evoke rocks, castle parapets, stairs and tombs, all harking back to Shakespeare's Elsinore in order to capture, in one image, the physical place and social milieu in which Hamlet both meditates upon and acts out his existential quest.

Figure 1.4 *Hamlet: a monologue* (1995). Photograph by T. Charles Erickson, courtesy of T. Charles Erickson

Wilson must have felt some qualms when he entered the world of drama with Shakespeare, the most canonical dramatist of them all. The experimental environment he had known in New York in the 1960s and 1970s had not equipped him for such a step, anymore than had his own writing; and a whole host of internationally authoritative productions of Shakespeare from Asia as well as Europe, many of them recent, had enriched the world's theatre culture, a fact he could not ignore. Furthermore, Shakespeare, just like Chekhov and the dramatists whom he was to stage afterwards, was part of literary history and was frequently referred to as 'literature'. This was something Wilson could not accept since, for him, the autonomy of a production was beyond question: a production was a work in and of itself, not merely an animated text. He faced an additional difficulty, for Shakespeare, like the 'classics' in general, had been co-opted by realistic performance conventions, which were at odds with his aesthetics. On the other hand, Wilson fully recognised that a 'great' text asserted its own authority. It was, in his words to actors repeatedly across the years, a 'rock', and, as such, it could withstand whatever he might do to it.

Quite likely, Wilson's blend of respect and iconoclasm as regards 'great' texts was born out of collaboration with Müller, who had plundered them for his own ends; and, arguably, he had learned from Müller's word power, by osmosis, as was typical of him, the power of the word. Also, another kind of experience of texts had come his way. By the time of *Hamlet*, Wilson had become a director of opera whose libretti borrow their structural and story elements from drama. He had seen this full well when he directed his first mainstream opera at La Scala in Milan in 1987. It was *Salomé* by Richard Strauss, its libretto based on the play by Oscar Wilde. That the production was commissioned by La Scala, the most prestigious of European opera houses, testifies to the credit Wilson had accumulated by then in Europe.

In short, Wilson became acquainted with dramatic texts through various channels. Since his approach to them is discussed in the following chapter, it suffices to cite chronologically the relevant works up to 2006: Ibsen's *When We Dead Awaken* (1991), Büchner's *Danton's Death* (1992), Ibsen's *The Lady From the Sea* (1998, adapted by Sontag), Strindberg's *Dream Play* (1998), Büchner's *Woyzeck* (2000, albeit as music theatre), Chekhov's *Three Sisters* (2001) and Ibsen's *Peer Gynt* (2005). In 2004, Wilson directed a selection of fables by seventeenth-century French poet La Fontaine, which he metamorphosed into a fine hybrid of poetry and drama. In the process, La Fontaine's animals were transformed into animal–human characters of separate mini-scripts, each adding up to the larger playscript of the production.

MUSIC THEATRE

Word, sound and music have gone together in Wilson's *oeuvre* since *A Letter for Queen Victoria*. And his work is always musical, relying on rhythm, pitch, tone, timbre, intonation, volume, cadence and pause, even when a sound is isolated, like the sound of glass being smashed intermittently in *Orlando*. Nevertheless, a large number of his productions involve music to such an extent that they must be called music theatre. They essentially fall into four groups: avant-garde opera, court opera, folk-rock and what is usually known as 'grand' opera to distinguish it from operetta and other musicals.

The first group gathers *Einstein on the Beach*, the Rome section of *the CIVIL warS*, and a later Wilson–Glass collaboration, *Monsters of Grace* (1998). *Monsters* is a self-conscious experiment in 3-D vision set to digital music. Its music hammers away while spectators, in a rather witty throwback to 1950s movies, sit in front of a screen wearing 3-D glasses and watching computer-animated objects (dishes of food, a carving knife) zoom out at them and vanish into nowhere. For all its efforts, this opera is dull, but it demonstrates that Wilson is able to turn his hand to just about anything. The second group, that of court opera, comprises Charpentier's *Médeé* at the Lyon Opéra in 1984 and *Orphée et Euridyce* and *Alceste*, both by Gluck, at the Châtelet Theatre in Paris in 1999. The stylisation of this genre suits Wilson's formalised aesthetic.

The third group, Wilson's folk-rock music theatre, is made up of five productions: *The Black Rider* (1990); *Alice* (1992, based on *Alice in Wonderland* by Lewis Carroll); *Time Rocker* (1996, a fantasia on the science fiction of H.G. Wells); *POEtry* (2000, devised from the poems of Edgar Allen Poe, as the pun of the title suggests) and *Woyzeck* (cross-referenced earlier). All but *Woyzeck* were sponsored and premiered by the Thalia Theatre in Hamburg, *Woyzeck* by the Betty Nansen Theatre in Copenhagen. These pieces celebrate a raw kind of 'Americanness' that Wilson cherishes, and his choice of collaborators is also evidence of the pull of his roots. Tom Waits, the quintessence of home-spun 'popular' art combined with folk 'wisdom', wrote the music and lyrics for *The Black Rider*, *Alice* and *Woyzeck*, the last two with his partner Kathleen Brennan.

Burroughs, a predecessor of this 'folk'-type 'Americanness' as well as of hippies, wrote bits of text and several songs for *The Black Rider*. Lou Reed, founder of the 1960s rock group Velvet Underground, composed the music for *Time Rocker* and *POEtry*.

The Black Rider was revived in London in 2004, renewing Wilson's contact with the offbeat all-American culture generated during his youth. The production now featured Marianne Faithfull, a British icon of the 1960s who had hung around in the American underground and/or 'junkie' scene and had known Burroughs. Music, as for the other pieces cited, was played live and in full blast. In this version, *The Black Rider* toured to San Francisco and Sydney. In 2006, it was revived with another cast in Los Angeles, the site of old wounds received by Wilson more than 20 years before.

The Black Rider, like *Einstein* before it, became something of a cult production in Europe where it toured extensively during the early 1990s. Based on the 1811 tale *Die Freischütz* (*The Free-Shooter*) and Thomas de Quincey's 1823 *The Fatal Marksman*, which was inspired by the same tale, it tells of Wilhelm's bargain with the Devil to sell his soul for seven magic bullets that never fail to hit their target. Wilhelm thus becomes a good hunter, winning Käthchen's father's approval for her hand in marriage. However, on his wedding day, he mistakenly shoots his bride with the last bullet reserved by the Devil for his own use. Wilhelm goes mad. Burroughs associates the bullets with drugs and, although he jokingly compares Wilhelm's inevitable downfall with drug abuse ('just like marywanna leads to heroin'), he nevertheless encodes his past addiction to opium in his innuendoes. Moreover, he draws an implicit parallel between himself and Wilhelm, having accidentally shot his own wife while high on drugs.

Since *The Black Rider* also became something of a prototype for Wilson's subsequent folk-rock productions, a summary of its features is useful. The Wilson–Waits–Burroughs trio caught the German tale's sinister edge, but added comic-satirical overtones and tragic undertones to it. Waits's score is raucous, splicing music in a fairground style with cabaret in the style of Kurt Weill mixed with elements of jazz.

Wilson's structure is a matter of layered contrasts, drawn from numerous sources: the fair (a barker opens the show to a roll of drums with 'Laaaadies and Gentlemen, step right up!'); circus (clown-like make-up, mimicry and movement); cabaret (including the Devil – 'Pegleg' in the production – as a high-camp master of ceremonies and 'artiste' on a swing; 1930s-type transvestite numbers, and echoes of Weill and Brecht's *Threepenny Opera*); German expressionist silent movies (particularly *The Cabinet of Dr Calagari*); opera (mock arias and a subversion of Weber's 1821 opera *Die Freischütz*, which is based on the story); animated cartoons (especially evident in forest and hunting scenes); American vaudeville (in countless steps and gestures); Broadway musicals (in song-and-dance duos between Wilhelm and Käthchen – tap-dance phrases included – and in rodeo-style solos recalling *Oklahoma*); variety shows (dancers covered by placards dance in front of the fire curtain, which drops occasionally, interrupting the dramatic action). Bourroughs's texts are laconic and dry, as are Waits's songs, by contrast with Wilson's opulent stage.

Nostalgia for his origins may well have prompted Wilson to mount this first of his folk-rock pieces, which, although twinning North American and European cultures, are fundamentally American. His productions of grand opera, on the other hand, are fundamentally European. Opera, the fourth group of Wilson's music theatre, is his most concentrated group, numbering some 20 productions from 1987 to 2006, a staggering amount by any standard. This makes Wilson very much an opera director, which comes as a surprise to spectators accustomed to thinking of him as a *theatre* director exclusively. It is just as surprising for those who wrap him up in a time warp with *Einstein* in the 1970s avant-garde. And yet Wilson's opera range is wide, covering composers as different as Mozart (*The Magic Flute*, 1991) and Wagner. His production of Wagner's mammoth *Ring* tetralogy began at the Zurich Opera in 2000 and spanned several years. It was reprised in its entirety for the Châtelet Theatre's 2005–06 opera season as a co-production between the two theatres.

France launched Wilson's directing career internationally, but played a similarly important role in his development as a director of opera, providing him with finance, staff and theatres that were sole producers or co-producers of his experiments. Experiments are precisely what they were as he transferred his theatre methods to a genre mired in sacrosanct traditions and in complex infrastructures reluctant to let them go. The prestige Wilson had acquired in France since the early 1970s eventually won him the confidence of opera houses, and the early 1990s saw his opera-directing career really take off. His ascent was helped along by an invitation from the Ministry of Culture to inaugurate the Opéra Bastille in Paris in 1989 for the bicentenary of the French Revolution.

Wilson was asked to stage a concert of French music in the new house that had been François Mitterrand's very own special project – the summit of his government's cultural policy in which Jack Lang's idea of 'culture for everybody' had played a crucial part. The Opéra Bastille was where opera was to lose its elitist image and become a democratic art.

Among Mitterrand and Lang's strategies to achieve this goal was the provision of generous subsidies for tickets, thus lowering the cost to spectators. To this day, ticket prices at the Bastille are some of the lowest in Western Europe. Mitterrand was a shrewd politician, and, although accused of opportunism in his attempts to democratise art, he had a genuine commitment to national glory. He bequeathed the opera house to the nation on the eve of the bicentenary, initiating a spate of official celebrations conducted in the desired pomp and circumstance of the occasion. No one could ignore the significance of the government's commission to Wilson, and it certainly gained him extra international standing. Two years later, his production of *The Magic Flute* appeared at the Bastille, the first of several opera productions backed by the two houses comprising the National Paris Opera, the new Bastille and the old Garnier. If Wilson asserted at the time of the *CIVIL warS* that the United States needed a cultural policy, the opportunities consolidated for him by the bicentenary could do nothing but confirm his belief.

Finally, there is *I La Galigo*, a work of music theatre that does not fit any of the groups mentioned earlier. It is based on the *Sureq Galigo*, a creation myth of the Bugis people who are an ethnic minority living on Sulawesi, an island to the north of Bali. Lasting five years, the project was promoted by the Bali Purnati Centre for the Arts as 'an unusual opportunity to serve Indonesian arts, artists, scholarship and scholars on an international platform' (*I La Galigo*, 2004: 108). It involved musicians and dancers from the whole Indonesian archipelago, although they came primarily from South Sulawesi, the home of the epic. Wilson's collaborators rehearsed and co-ordinated the work in Indonesia while he was otherwise engaged in Europe. *I La Galigo* was premiered in Singapore in 2004 before touring to Amsterdam, Lyon, Barcelona and Ravenna and, in 2005, to New York. The theatre and festival organisations of these cities had co-produced it, guaranteeing the 'international platform' considered necessary for preserving the *Sureq Galigo* from oblivion. The mechanisms of globalisation, while frequently harmful to indigenous cultures, do not appear, in this case, to have worked for neo-colonial or hegemonic ends.

The *Sureq Galigo* is a ritual in story-telling form, written and chanted in an archaic language to music and dance. *I La Galigo* respects these performance traditions, as reconstructed by Wilson's Indonesian collaborators while he lightly etched his own conceptions of performance over them. The result is an incomparably harmonious production in which ancient lore becomes a subtle and exquisite modern work of Bugis culture, touched by Wilson's hand, but not possessed by it. By now Wilson had indeed been on a long artistic journey since his loft dances in the 1960s, and he had come a long way from Texas.

2

METHOD, ELEMENTS
AND PRINCIPLES

The ambition, scope and diversity of Wilson's work are evident from the preceding chapter, even when the list is incomplete. Can such a hetero-geneous range be underpinned by the unifying intellectual construction that is theory? Wilson's crossovers are an early and still leading example of a practice that has become the norm in the twenty-first century. But are they a consequence of theoretical precepts, or did they emerge from being done without theoretical design?

Wilson has not produced a master body of thought let alone manifestos, like Tadeusz Kantor (another visual artist of the stage), or conversational books, like Peter Brook. Brook, as is clear from his remarks about his theatre, has a pragmatist's mistrust of theory, and Wilson, like Brook, keeps theory at arm's length. It is too verbal for his fundamentally visual and kinetic sensibility and, as Wilson has repeated for the past 40 years, he works intuitively, although not in a random fashion: 'I don't like things to be done incidentally. Something is here because something else is there. But it isn't necessarily conscious in my work. That's why I say I work very intuitively' (Friedl, 1982: 58). One of his earlier collaborators, light designer Beverly Emmons observes that he 'thinks of things as he goes along and quite often he doesn't know just what he needs until it is all there in the theatre' (Shyer, 1989: 200). To watch him work today is to see that he generally has a strong sense of what he might be after, much of it now backed by his considerable experience.

The point of the work for him is in the doing, which is why he has a method, is methodical, and dislikes excessive discussion, particularly in rehearsals.

A WORKSHOP METHOD

FROM STORYBOARD TO VISUAL BOOK

The fact that Wilson does not have a theory does not mean that he does not think. His interviews are where he reflects upon his practice, despite his shyness of words, and observations taken from them for this chapter are essentially the thought basis of his performance work. Moreover, there are various ways of thinking – by visual, musical and other non-verbal means, with the body (especially the case of dancers), and in silence. Wilson thinks in all these ways and starts with his 'storyboards' (the term from the film technique of sketching scenes to be shot), which he appears to have used for the first time for *Einstein*. He was soon to call them his 'visual books'. Everything sketched in them, scene by scene, usually with texts beside or below his drawings, are a support for the preparation of his productions as well as their actual staging. The spaces and shapes of his scenes are configurations rather than illustrations, but they nevertheless summarise in images the overall structure of a work, how long it will be, how scenes will look and what will happen in them. Wilson elaborates:

> how different scenes can relate to one another, whether there might be recitatives or something spoken, a duet, or some songs. I do it with drawings to see the construction, to see how the story is told visually, how the architecture looks in time and space.
>
> (Enright, 1994: 16)

The 'visual books' are Wilson's first step towards what, in the same interview, he calls the 'visual book' (collective noun) which, he believes, Western theatre has not adequately developed: 'Shakespeare, Goethe, Schiller, Molière, Racine, Tennessee Williams are men who wrote words, who wrote literature for the theatre' (ibid.: 18). Contemporary actor training has followed suit, becoming 'so intellectual' that it neglects the simplest techniques of the body – sitting on a chair, walking on the stage; and it cannot begin to compare with Balinese theatre training where there are 'three-to-four hundred movements of the eyes alone' (ibid.). Wilson's 'visual book', then, can be paraphrased, from the immediate context of his discussion, as 'gestural language':

> We just haven't developed a language. If you look at the classical theatre in Japan – Noh, Kabuki or whatever – as much time is spent on learning a gesture as in the sound they produce or the poem that's being spoken or the story that's being told. How do you stand in a Noh play?... How do you pick up a fan, how do you hold it... what is the line of the finger in space?... How do you place a motion? They have a theatrical language developed through the body that is simply lacking in our theatre. We've developed it in dance.
>
> (Ibid.)

There is an echo here of Ariane Mnouchkine's call for an 'art of the actor' that typifies 'the great traditional Eastern forms, whether Japanese, Indian, Balinese' and is antithetical to the Western 'art of the text' (Shevtsova, 1995–96: 8). And, indeed, Wilson's admiration not only for Japanese, but also Balinese classical theatre (with less impact on his style than on Mnouchkine's) led him, on the one hand, to Suzushi Hanayagi, who was trained in the jiuta-mai school of traditional dance (Morey and Pardo, 2003: 99) and, on the other, to *I La Galigo*. Here scenes honour a rich performance history: birds fly on sticks (Figure 2.1); cats prowl, with huge hoops for tails; men 'row' across the seas on haunches across the floor – all with agile bodies, light feet and nimble fingers. These graceful scenes co-exist harmoniously with the hieratic positions and gestures typical of Wilson's approach. Take, as an example, how the Princess of the story gives birth, the latter implied by means of veils unwinding from her body (Figure 2.2). The closing scene in which the ancient rice goddess indicates the passage of time with her fan (performed by a 77-year old Indonesian master) is the epitome of simplicity, and a stunning demonstration of how you 'hold' a fan.

Despite the touch of 'Orientalism' in Wilson's discussion of Eastern performance – and aspects of his theatre echo the East–West 'inter-cultural' paradigm of the 1980s and 1990s – Wilson is not in the least interested in exoticism or appropriation. His goal is to establish a gestural language adequate to his productions, and he keeps this language in mind as he draws his visual books. Its most specific details are determined only when they are tried and tested, often innumerably, in the real time

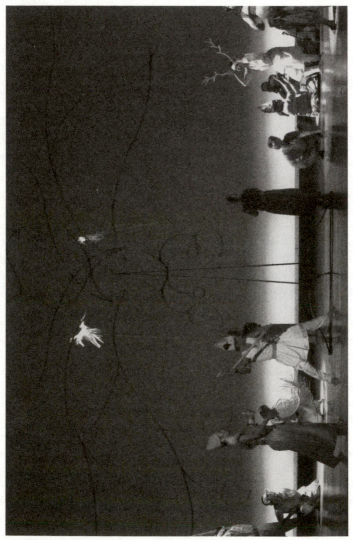

Figure 2.1
I La Galigo (2004).
Photograph by
Pavel Antonov,
courtesy of Pavel
Antonov

Figure 2.2
I La Galigo (2004).
Photograph by
Kim Cheong and
Ung Ruey Loon,
courtesy of
Esplanade
Theatres on the
Bay/Singapore
and Change
Performing Arts

and space afforded by rehearsals. Wilson may not have a theory to check or prove, but his work with everyone during the production process is meticulous and exacting.

The account to follow, while necessarily referring to interviews with Wilson, draws on his productions, as it must, since Wilson's method and its principles are embodied in them by verbal and non-verbal means. The idea of 'embodiment' is especially apt for Wilson because he has never stopped thinking of his work as dance, the most corporeal, in-the-body art of them all. And the principle of dance affects all the elements that he uses to such an extent that nothing is ever quite static, not even objects, let alone light, that moving light which has made him a light designer unparalleled among peers. My examples from his productions lead into, or are corroborated by, interviews with Wilson.

WORKSHOPS

Preparations for a project usually start a number of years ahead, Wilson claiming that he generally needs a lot of time, especially for assemblages like *Death Destruction and Detroit* and *the CIVIL warS*, to 'gather ideas, information, find a theme, a gesture, a text, a colour, a language, a word, lighting' (Friedl, 1982: 55). Since the 1990s, and particularly since he stepped up his work on European classics, preparation time has been reduced, usually to one or two years in advance, and by prior consultation with his team whose members excel at their respective tasks. Some have worked consistently with him for decades. Others come in and out, and still others collaborate on several projects in a row and then do not return, usually for circumstantial reasons. Ann-Christin Rommen, who has been Wilson's directing assistant since the Cologne section of *the CIVIL warS*, is a permanent member of his team, and is sometimes billed as his co-director. Michael Galasso, who wrote the music for *Peer Gynt*, is an example of the second type of participant and has contributed to specific projects since *The Life and Times of Joseph Stalin*. Monica Ohlsson from the Stadsteatern in Stockholm, who was Wilson's dramaturg for *Three Sisters* and *A Dream Play* as well as *Peer Gynt*, is an example of the third type. The essential point is that Wilson's collaborative work involves selection from a pool of co-workers according to project. This kind of team system is quite differ-ent from the tight-knit, ongoing collaboration of an ensemble company such as the Maly Drama Theatre of St Petersburg, taking the most striking contrast (Shevtsova, 2004: 36–60).

Once a work has been decided or commissioned, it usually goes through three phases, starting with what Wilson calls a 'table workshop' – a meeting generally of Wilson, Rommen and a dramaturg, scenographer, costume designer and composer, others included when necessary. They talk through the piece so as to map out its narrative content. In the case of *Peer Gynt*, for instance, produced by Det Norske Teatret in Oslo, Rommen and Ohlsson summarised each scene on the lines of 'Peer does this, he says that, his mother (or someone else) replies and then this happens with such and such consequences'. The bare bones of the story prompted Wilson to ask various questions – for instance, where x event happened, when it happened, what time of day it happened and how many people were involved. As a summary proceeds and more questions are asked, Wilson draws, visualising his thoughts. Hence, of course, the idea of the 'visual books'.

Wilson's first response is to envisage the space structure for each scene and whether it will be shaped by a painted drop, reproduced photograph, scrim or cut-out in some highly resistant material that will slide in from the wings or drop down from the flies to configure it. Details of time might appear through shading or hard thick strokes. Details of setting are almost never drawn pictorially in the manner of landscape painting. Thus the mountains of *Peer Gynt* are roughly marked by strong geometrical patterns. Indeterminate figures appear occasionally, as in the visual book for *Peer Gynt*, to indicate their relation to the space. However, spatial and movement relations between performers are defined during rehearsals, where Wilson adjusts a position, stance, head, hand or whatever aspect of the gestural vocabulary needs to be put into focus. It was evident in the rehearsals of *Peer Gynt* that some of his drawings were like a mnemonic, reminding him of what he had initially imagined, although the development of scenes occurred only as he worked with the actors.

Apart from producing the visual books, the table workshop is crucial for the dramaturg whose task is to excise a text while ensuring that its narrative foundations remain more or less intact. Dialogue is shortened and some of it omitted, but decisions about cuts are a two-way process depending on the verbal summaries of his collaborators and the cues that Wilson gives back to them via his visual book; the hard part, for the dramaturg, comes after the table workshop in that all further textual adjustments rely on the play of the performers and Wilson's readjustments to it. The designers begin their research during the table workshop.

Discussions might also be about props and whether and when they should be still or move, Wilson's drawings providing cues, once again. The composer starts thinking about possible kinds of music or sound effects. This activity is not meant to unify the production but to give every contributor a starting point so that nothing in it turns out to be incidental.

The various contributions are eventually put together coherently. However, Wilson treats the elements concerned as separate entities right from the start so that, in his words, 'they don't risk illustrating each other mutually, are not dependent on each other' (Grillet and Wilson, 1992: 13). By respecting their autonomy, Wilson accords them equal importance. Wilson remarks:

> In the European tradition, the text is the most important element on the stage. In my theatre all the elements are equal: the space, the light, the actors, the sound, the texts, the costumes, and the props. I think that is something Brecht tried to bring to the German theatre, too.
>
> (quoted in Teschke, 1999: 14)

A good seven years earlier, Heiner Müller had also evoked Brecht to illuminate Wilson's practice, arguing that 'the essential thing about Wilson's theatre is the separation of the elements, a dream of Brecht's' (quoted in ibid.).

The second phase involves casting (in some cases also finalising casting issues with the producers) and the first workshop with the actors. Auditions look rather mechanical. Actors are typically asked to walk, sit, speak a short text, sing a few lines and repeat a movement pattern demonstrated by Wilson. Rommen claims that 'there, you can see everything' (7 February 2005). Months can pass before the first actor workshop, which lasts two or three weeks and which Wilson, harking back to his earliest work, conducts as a 'silent play', without any dialogue, but frequently with music. The actors know the text in question and sometimes have performed it in conventional text-based theatre, as was the case, for example, of the actor who performed the old Peer Gynt. (Wilson had three actors for the role, inspired by Ibsen's organisation of the play around three age-frames for Peer – young, middle-aged and old.) The aim of the silent play is to familiarise the actors with Wilson's performance language, which they learn as dancers learn a fixed choreography and in much the same kind of repetitive, routine manner. While they work in this way, Rommen and the dramaturg usually note where dialogue is to be inserted and how long it should be.

Talk during the actor workshop is explanatory, basically providing hooks into Wilson's universe. After all, being asked to gesticulate and move in the impersonal, impassive Wilson mode – robotic, when performed perfunctorily, graceful and meaningful, when with conviction – is not most actors' idea of acting, and can be particularly daunting when actors have not seen a Wilson production, not even on video. Wilson, who is perfectly aware of this, attempts to connect his approach with something familiar to them. Take, for example, his remarks in the first workshop for *Ozeanflug* (*Oceanflight*), Brecht's radio play staged by Wilson at the Berliner Ensemble in 1998. The idea to mount the piece for the Brecht centennial had come from Heiner Müller shortly before his death in 1995. Holger Teschke, the dramaturg for the production, writes:

> The work with the actors began. Wilson explained his concept to the team. When explaining his ideas for the piece, Wilson spoke of Brecht and Weigel, whom he saw play *The Mother* in Paris. He spoke of the simplicity and clarity of her movements. He told of his friendship with Heiner Müller, recounted anecdotes from their work together on the German part of [*the*] *CIVIL warS* and on *Hamletmachine* in Hamburg and New York. He also described his conception of the theatre.
>
> (1999: 14)

Müller had been associated with the Berliner Ensemble since Brecht's time and had also been its Artistic Director, so Wilson's personal recollections were meaningful to the assembled company. Unfortunately, Teschke does not mention the silent play crucial to this phase.

The first workshop is also when developments since the table discussions are tested and reviewed. Teschke remarks that during this period for *Ozeanflug*

> stage designs were laid out and partly set up for the fist time, the lighting facilities of the theatre were looked over and tested, and music and text versions were discussed and developed. All this went on simultaneously in various workrooms and rehearsal spaces at many tables, using many stage models, and sometimes full-scale mock-up stage walls from the set; the process might seem somewhat chaotic to the outsider.
>
> (Ibid.: 13–14)

This is an intensive version of the 'business as usual' of theatre making, compounded by the exceptionally high expectations of the contributors, who work independently along their respective tracks and yet, paradoxically, have to be on the right track to 'fit' into the 'textured arrangement' constituting a production (my phrase in the preceding chapter). Their input, in other words, is not so much organic as expert; and their expertise guarantees their independence. The paradox independence/consensus has become such a strong feature of Wilson's method in the past decade – capped by a remarkable efficiency (despite seeming *and* real chaos) – that it suggests the corporate model referred to in the preceding chapter. Which is not to deny the artistry – frequently superlatively imaginative – of the productions that are finally made.

The third phase involves what can be called different 'moments', starting with the second workshop with actors. The time between the actor workshops varies – for instance, nine months between the first and second for *Peer Gynt*, seven for *Ozeanflug*. By then, the actors are expected to have memorised the movement score and internalised its tones, rhythms and phrasing. 'Score' here intentionally echoes Meyerhold's term (which originates with Stanislavsky) for the idea that movements can be as precise as musical notes and follow their intrinsic logic without any recourse to 'natural' behaviour or to psychological justification for it. Wilson's procedure, although not formulated by him in these terms, can be seen to be on a similar line of thought, which is not surprising given the affinity of his practice with the modernist practices of the early twentieth century. The main purpose of the second actor workshop is to connect the silent and the verbal work and adjust them to each other. Any necessary textual alterations are made here by the dramaturg (and dialogue is re-inserted if too much of it had been cut) for what becomes the 'final' text by the end of the workshop.

The next 'moment', which usually runs on from the second actor workshop, is the actual production and rehearsal time, and lasts from three to five–six weeks, depending on the contractual agreements between Wilson and the hosting theatre. The lighting, although anticipated to some extent by the visual book and the workshops, is really done during this third phase. There is no fixed formula for how the team's division of labour will go into gear. Wilson, for example, spent little time on the text for *Peer Gynt*: Ohlsson's revisions held fast, and the actors had a firm grip on their lines. By contrast, Teschke notes for *Ozeanflug* that Wilson spent 'an unusual amount of time working on the text, continually searching for new solutions to do justice to the language of Brecht's learning play for the radio' (1999: 15). Teschke also observes that Rommen 'worked through the scenic constellations with the actors' (ibid.), whereas, as far as I could tell from the rehearsals of *Peer Gynt*, that responsibility fell primarily to Wilson. Rommen, for her part, had come before these rehearsals 'to place the text with the actors so it could live inside those movements [established by Wilson's silent work] and make sense' (7 February 2005).

In general, Rommen works with the actors rather like a *maître de danse* who fulfils what the choreographer of a ballet company has set; and, in this role, she sometimes replaces Wilson during the second workshop. The third phase dovetails into the production 'proper' in that Wilson likes to arrange a preview week before the planned premiere. Some preview performances are free (*Peer Gynt* in Oslo) while others are sold (*The Black Rider* in London), this depending on the producing theatre's policy. Of course, the presence of spectators affects the performers, and Wilson uses the feedback loop between stage and audience, when he can, to fine-tune details, including details of lighting.

Whatever the variations to the plan of action might be, the autonomy of team members, as they carry out their research, presupposes collective faith in the long-term outcome, as does their co-operation when they converge. The well-known Italian critic Franco Qaudri's short article in the programme of *I La Galigo* sheds some light on this meeting of aesthetics, authority, division of labour, organisation and conviction:

> For many months Artistic Director Restu I. Kusumaningrum searched through all of Indonesia, choosing hundreds of dancers educated from childhood in the traditional forms to offer for a final selection to be made by Wilson, who led them through movement variations based on his work, as would happen in the workshop begun in 2001. As Restu herself tells it, 'The maestro came at regular intervals, for a few very intense days, in which he reviewed the work he had done previously and adding new touches, often with a fantastic surreal flavour, while never losing sight of the traditional base.'
>
> (2004: 69)

'Final selection' and 'maestro' indicate unequivocally the authority invested in Wilson. Nevertheless, it would be a mistake to believe that

Restu was simply a cog in a machine, her efforts subsumed under Wilson's aesthetic 'vision'. In the five years of preparation required, she exercised her initiative as much as the 'Javanese master' did, 'who chose historic music from the Indonesian repertory, paying close attention to the religious traditions, to which he then gave a contemporary twist' (ibid.). Autonomy necessarily had to come into play to bring the production to successful completion. Quadri says as much:

> With each part so thoroughly researched, the show has therefore been able to come together extremely quickly in the last three weeks in Singapore's Esplanade Theatre, where the mounting accumulation of pieces, despite their complexity, were fused into something extremely natural, thanks to the magic of imagination.
>
> (Ibid.)

The creative tension between the 'part so thoroughly researched' and the whole, between the team members and the director, and between their work and his 'vision' is resolved in the production. This kind of tension is characteristic of all collaborative work regardless of how its processes differ according to each collaborative group. Wilson cannot escape it and, if anything, his total commitment to the idea that art supersedes all other wants and desires swings the balance in his favour, giving him the final say in the details of the production understood to be a coherent whole. His conviction that art is a supreme value in itself is anything but postmodernist, and this attitude joins him to twentieth-century modernism, once again. His nearest links in this respect are Edward Gordon Craig's devotion to Art, which Wilson matches, Craig's ideal of the all-encompassing creator, which Wilson modifies by his dovetailed team approach, and Craig's goal of liberation from texts through movement (Craig, 1978), which Wilson realises in his 'dance plays' and 'silent operas'.

ELEMENTS AND PRINCIPLES

ARCHITECTURE, SPACE, TIME

'I do not have a message. What I do is an architectural arrangement' (Lesschaeve, 1977: 217), Wilson told his interviewer shortly after the opening of *Einstein on the Beach*, adding that his objective for the theatre was the 'architectural arrangement in space and time' achieved by Cunningham for dance (ibid.: 224). Wilson's phrase and its variations over the years (among them 'constructions in time and space'; Holmberg, 1996: 80) draw attention to how 'architecture', 'construction', 'structure', 'composition' and 'form' are virtually synonymous for him. His collocation of terms explains Wilson's apparently anomalous use of 'architecture' not for a building or a design, but for such varied phenomena as counterpoint in music, shafts of light, lines traced in space by moving bodies or the placement of props – all 'form' in some sense of the word. At times his vocabulary is simply cryptic. When, for instance, he asks actors to be 'formal', he means that they should stylise their voices, movements and gestures. When he insists that his productions are 'formal', he means that their style is his foremost concern: his productions *are*, and are not 'about' anything. Wilson is perhaps clearest about his approach when he speaks of Cézanne whose principle of composition (or 'architecture') along the horizontal, vertical and diagonal lines of perspective corresponds with his own:

> Cézanne is my favourite painter. My work is closer to him than to any other artist. My production of *Hamletmachine* is like a Cézanne painting in its architecture. Cézanne simplified and purified forms to reveal classical structure and composition. I learned everything from Cézanne, his use of colour, light, the diagonal, and space – how to use the centre and the edges. His images are not framed by the boundaries.
>
> (quoted in Holmberg, 1996: 79)

And Cézanne's structured but spacious-looking canvas is Wilson's model for the stage. 'I'm a visual artist', says Wilson, 'I think spatially' (ibid.: 77). However, the stage also provides him with a temporal dimension – after all, a performance has continuity – and this is the 'time' in relation to 'space' of his 'architectural arrangement'.

Given his preoccupation with visual composition, it is not surprising that Wilson should appreciate the proscenium arch above all other playing spaces (Obenhaus, 1985). The proscenium offsets his structures (or 'architecture') and provides them with a frame without closing them in. According to Wilson, the proscenium has the additional virtue of allowing people to *hear* better. The paradox of hearing better in a space of seeing makes sense when we realise that, for Wilson, seeing and hearing, although separate activities, reinforce each other: the high resolution of the one – the picture in the proscenium – enhances the quality of the other. Wilson's belief in the power of the proscenium to bring out the senses indicates why he rejected found spaces for avant-garde productions like *Freud* and *Einstein*, contrary to the preference for such spaces of the avant-garde of the time.

Cézanne also showed Wilson how an impression of monumentality could be created through the play of geometric shapes, planes and lines. Even so, Wilson's concern is to give his monumental structures some air – like Craig, who built huge screens for his production of *Hamlet* at the Moscow Art Theatre in 1912 (Innes, 1998: 163–71). Craig's screens attempted to shape space by combining what looked like weight with lightness, the latter made possible by the fact that the screens could move. Wilson's moving vast 'pillars' and 'walls' have a similar effect, making space mobile, dynamic. Yet his geometric constructions are so imposing that, overall, they recall not so much Craig as Adolph Appia whose designs for Wagner's operas he had studied when preparing *Parsifal* for 1982, a project that was cancelled (Shyer, 1989: 138; Wilson, 2002: 427). Appia's stage designs foreground tightly contained mass. Wilson contrasts blocs of mass – columns representing trees in *The Forest* or tombs in *Aida* – with open space around them. Wilson, like Appia, explores scenographically the three dimensions of architecture, and he is particularly interested in the tension between this three-dimensional space and the two-dimensional space of pictures and backdrops, that is, between depth and surface, which is evident in most of his productions after the early 1980s.

Space, Wilson insists, is not merely 'there', to be taken for granted. It must be *inhabited* by actors and so they must think about the space they are in before anything else (Holmberg, 1996: 202). An example from his production of *Peer Gynt* illustrates this point well. It comes from Act IV, scene iv, as designated by Wilson's visual book (Act IV without a numbered scene in Ibsen's text). Ibsen's stage direction reads 'a rocky place overlooking the desert, with a cave, and a ravine to one side' (1980: 125). Wilson's visual book repeats only 'a rocky place overlooking the desert'. This line is accompanied by a sketch of three uneven boulder-looking shapes in an elongated triangle on the ground.

Wilson saw 'the desert' as a lunar landscape, which materialised on the stage as a strange, open space lit in a deep luminous blue to suggest moonlight. During the first of the stage rehearsals the actor moved about the 'rocks' without feeling the space's liminal quality until Wilson suggested that he move among them like a curious child. Wilson soon decided that the horizontal shapes looked uninteresting and, as such, could hardly inspire the actor to create the sense of playful mystery he was after. Consequently, the papier mâché 'rocks', which looked deceptively heavy, were suspended in the air at slightly different heights, the glitter sprinkled on them catching the light. This helped the actor to inhabit the space and really make it his own as he changed position and gazed like a child – here under one hanging boulder, there vertically beside another, somewhere else at a diagonal (Figure 2.3). Prompted by Wilson, he added a humorous touch to the nocturne's magic, and, by inhabiting the atmospheric space in a non-atmospheric way, he also realised the principle of contradiction of such importance to Wilson.

The contradiction accentuated in this scene is evident in all of Wilson's work, but is especially striking in his opera productions primarily because of the antithesis between the richness of operatic music and his austere *mise en scène*, which governs everything else. *Pelléas and Mélisande* (1998), for instance, is built around a series of contradictions starting from the initial one between Debussy's highly evocative orchestral score

Figure 2.3 *Peer Gynt* (2005). Photograph by Lesley Leslie-Spinks, courtesy of Lesley Leslie-Spinks

and Wilson's spartan stage: the dream world of Maeterlinck's play (which is used by Debussy for his libretto) awash with mysterious innuendoes versus the intimations of threat and violence of the production's nightmare world; the singers' pure singing versus their menacing movements, and so forth.

The scene that encapsulates these contradictions concerns Mélisande and her husband Golaud who loves her, but is jealous of her affectionate relationship with his younger brother Pelléas. She walks in a flowing movement in a semi-circle, while he paces behind her like a stalker stalking his victim. Their duet is essentially a dance of murderous love, and the scene's sinister undertow is heightened, together with its dance-like quality, when Mélisande and Golaud come together for a trio with Pelléas, the latter ending his sequence in an arabesque on the floor. This dark drama is performed to gentle music in hauntingly subdued light. Wilson's principle of contradiction operates in the entire opera, as else-where in his work, on the juxtaposition and counterpoint of contrary elements: a baroque candelabra on a rock, he says, is far more effective than one on a baroque table (Obenhaus, 1985); and his appreciation of startling incongruity is close to French poet Lautréamont's definition of beauty (which became a surrealist catch-cry) as 'the chance encounter of a sewing machine and an umbrella on a dissecting table' (in his *Les Chants de Maldoror*, 1868–70). The opera measures time as moment, duration, continuity and end – a process evident in all his theatre, which critics have attacked for being slow. Wilson retaliates:

> That's wrong. It's *not* in slow motion, it's in natural time. Most theatre deals with speeded-up time, but I use the kind of natural time in which its takes the sun to set, a cloud to change, a day to dawn. I give you time to reflect, to meditate about other things than those happening on the stage. I give you time and space in which to think.
>
> (*New York Times*, 2 December 1984)

'Think' is in the sense of 'reverie', and Wilson has insisted over the years that this kind of time allows spectators to find their 'mental landscape' (Schechner, 2003: 115). Their 'interior reflection' (Wilson in Holmberg, 1996: 162) – 'screen', as Wilson also frequently calls it – is stimulated by the exterior or 'sensory surface' (Sontag's terms) of the production, but can only be sustained by the 'special' time of the theatre where 'we can stretch time, we can compress it; we can do whatever we want' (Wilson in Schechner, 2003: 119). Whether deemed slow or not, Wilson's time determines the quality of scenes, the graceful transition between scenes, and the length of his productions, some of which, we have seen, are unusually long. Although Wilson occasionally speeds up time, just a little, he never lets go the sensation of savoured time that suffuses his productions and is communicated to audiences.

Nor does he ever relinquish the sense of timing he prizes so highly (Obenhaus, 1985). Timing is part of precision, and Wilson has his actors count time for a spoken line, movement or pause so that each can be the exact length, as well as produce the desired tone – comic, melodramatic or enchanting, among a range of them facilitated by accurate timing. The celebrated tap dancer Honni Coles, whom Wilson had persuaded to perform in *When We Dead Awaken*, said of rehearsals: 'It's just like vaudeville. It's all about practice, precision, rhythm and timing' (Holmberg, 1996: 138). During rehearsals of *The Black Rider* in London, probably the closest to a vaudeville that Wilson has ever come, he frequently referred the actors to Charlie Chaplin and Buster Keaton, champions of timing and of nuance of effect through timing for whom Wilson has special admiration.

ACTOR

Wilson's habitual term is 'actor' rather than 'performer', and his non-histrionic actor can only be compared to Craig's *Übermarionette*. The latter is not a puppet but Craig's defence against the actor as impersonator, or what he calls 'the actor the ventriloquist' (Craig, 1978: 41). Although Wilson did not borrow ideas from Craig, his measured, frequently trance-like performers, who place and pace their steps with great care, can be said to have realised Craig's ideal of 'the body in Trance – it will aim to clothe itself with a death-like Beauty while exhaling a living spirit' (ibid.).

The 'trance' sureness of step and gait is, for Wilson, an integral part of timing, which is why he asks actors to count as they move in his workshops. By doing so, they can incorporate not only a sense of time in their bodies, but also the sense of bodily ease with time that is associated with trance. These are techniques for stylising performance and are consistent with Wilson's aim to eliminate all signs of 'apparent emotion' (Lessachaeve, 1977: 224) from it. As a consequence, the actors *present* rather than express. The fact that Wilson gives priority to *presentation*, as distinct from expression, imitation or enactment, is crucial for our understanding what kind of actor he wants. And his non-emotive approach to acting is also tied up with his condemnation, like Craig's before him, of the theatre's preponderant 'naturalistic' pretence to copy life: 'Theatre for me is something totally artificial. If you don't accept it as something totally artificial, then it's a lie' (Wilson in Schechner, 2003: 120).

His rejection of naturalism does not stop Wilson from claiming that artificial acting must nevertheless be believable:

> One of the things I say to performers all the time is, 'I don't believe you. I don't believe you, Aida. You've got to do something to make me believe you'. Although its totally artificial, this voice, this movement, this stance, whatever the actor is doing, somehow has to be based on a truth. I touch this glass (*touches glass*). It's cool. That's truth. I touch my forehead (*touches his forehead*) and it's warmer. That's truth. I can act it, but it's got to be based on something that's true. I find that the more artificial it becomes, the closer it can get to a truth.
>
> (Ibid.)

Perhaps the only way to understand what seems here to be an impossible contradiction (the idea of artificial truth) is to remember Wilson's repeated dismissal of interpretation: 'My responsibility as an artist is to create, not to interpret' (Eco, 1993: 89). In other words, his notion of 'truth' is not a Stanislavskian interpretative truth. Wilson's 'truth' resides in the pronounced (artificial), formal (artificial) delivery of something that is just there, like the coolness of the glass to which he refers. Nothing special is to be made of this coolness.

By the same token, 'truth' comes from how the *actor* 'fill[s] in the form' – the pitch of a voice, the line of a movement, the angle of a stance – with 'inner feeling' (Wilson in Holmberg, 1996: 149). It comes, as well, from how the actor makes up his/her 'story' or 'subtext', which is integral to the 'interior acting style' (ibid.: 184) that Wilson prefers to exteriorised, expressive acting. (We need to be cautious. Wilson, who is not interested in 'character' as a psychosocial entity, uses 'subtext' in a non-Stanislavskian way.) Furthermore, he believes that a 'subtext can change every night. In that sense every performance is an improvisation'(ibid.: 149). Wilson fixes a form, not so as to subordinate the actor to it, but to hand it over to him/her, as this recent declaration confirms:

> Anyway, I give formal directions. I have never, ever in 30-something years of working in the theatre, I've never told an actor what to think. I've never told them what emotions to express. They're given these very, formal, strict movements and directions. Within that there is a freedom for the actors to fill in the form. The form is not important. The movement is not important. The structure that I give them is not important. It's how you fill in the form – that's what's important. Why is it that one woman dances *Giselle* the most beautifully? They're all doing the same steps. It's how she fills in the form.
>
> (Schechner, 2003: 126)

The boring part of his work, Wilson frequently observes during rehearsals, is giving actors a form. Their creative task is *filling* the form – with 'conviction' as I have called it earlier – so as to breathe individual 'living spirit' (Craig) into it. This is precisely why a pre-fixed solo score like *Orlando* changes quite radically in tone, temper and mood according to each performer. Isabelle Huppert explains her freedom vis-à-vis the established score by the fact that, instead of being caught between a 'text', a 'character' and 'great mise en scène' (she stresses that 'the actor often has trouble in the middle of all this'), she was a 'person . . . totally and completely myself . . . . The whole production comes from him, but he had me move in it as I wanted to' (Shevtsova, 1995b: 75).

Nonetheless, the actor must maintain 'a certain distance' (Enright, 1994: 17), which keeps the space open around him/her and between him/her and the spectator. This imperturbable actor (Craig's 'death-like Beauty') is distanced further still by light, colour, costume and make-up. Freed from emotion – or, more accurately, from emotional display – the actor is free to practice this or that formal aspect of play until it becomes a reflex. Wilson says:

> Well, I think in this age of technology that our only chance of beating the machine is to become mechanical, to become automatic. That's why in my theatre works you can't rehearse anything too much. And the more mechanical you become, the freer you become. It's like learning to ride a bicycle. The first time it may be awkward or difficult, like learning to play

Mozart on the piano, and in a sense we never learn. But the more we do it, the freer we become.

(Enright, 1994: 22)

Of course, the danger of becoming 'automatic', even when practice makes perfect, is becoming 'mechanical' in a negative way, that is, performing without living breath and without a subtext to nurture the freedom experienced within play. When Wilson directed *Les Fables de La Fontaine* at the Comédie Française in 2004, reviewers commented on the great difference between this exquisite work (which breathed, one might say, from within) and previous (unnamed) productions that they thought were trapped in his 'aesthetic grid' (*Figaroscope*, 11 February 2004), or 'engulfed in a formalism as brilliant as it was empty' (*Le Nouvel observateur*, 18 February 2004). These critics blamed what they believed had become Wilson's routine reproduction of a formula on his doing 'too much [too many shows] at once' (ibid.). They certainly had a point. Yet out of this overproduction (in which formulaic aspects *do* appear) came *Fables*, a marvel of wisdom, subtlety, simplicity, elegance and fun in an enchanted bestiary all the more magical for the masks – mouse, crow, frog, monkey, fox, deer, lion – worn by the actors to present their animals (Figure 2.4).

All kinds of masks and masking are visible in Wilson's productions. There are actual masks, as in *Fables* or *Peer Gynt*, where the trolls wear stunning comic-grotesque pig and other masks conceived by Jacques Reynaud, the production's costume designer; zany hairdos also function as masks (Figure 2.5). And there are the masks (or, rather, replacements for masks) of white make-up, which covers the actors' faces and bodies, and heavy make-up for the eyes and mouth. Such make-up – not used extensively by Wilson until the 1980s – is generally accentuated when 'characters' or situations are comical, camp or sinister, as in *The Black Rider*. Imperturbability and the feeling of distance emanating from the actors also function as masks. Animals are masks for human beings, as suggested on occasion in Wilson's silent operas, but which is explicit in the speaking animals of *Fables*, Wilson here following La Fontaine to the letter.

Emotions are masked, as well, in that they are conveyed indirectly by light, colour, costume and other means for keeping the histrionic actor's world at bay. Wilson's manner of displacing the actor's emotions away from the actor, transferring them to stage elements, which are intended,

Figure 2.4
*Les Fables de la
Fontaine* (2004).
Photograph by
Martine Franck,
courtesy of
Magnum Photos

Figure 2.5 *Peer Gynt* (2005). Photograph by Lesley Leslie-Spinks, courtesy of Lesley Leslie-Spinks

at the same time, to stimulate the emotions of spectators, is central to his conception of the actor as such. His principal mode of transferral is light. Some 15 years earlier, Marianne Hoppe, 'King Lear' in Wilson's production, was not impressed by how he diminished the role of the actor – indeed, mostly with light:

> This Wilson can't fool me. I started out at the Deutsches Theatre with Max Rheinhardt. I know what a director is. Wilson is not a director. He's a lighting designer. A Wilson actor runs here or there only because there's a change in the lights. On a Wilson stage, light pushes the actors around. Light is important, but in Shakespeare language is also important. I can speak the lines the way he wants, but I don't believe Shakespeare wrote the part of Lear to be recited by an autistic child.
>
> (Holmberg, 1996: 138)

King Lear may not have succeeded, despite Hoppe's remarkable abilities, but *Fables* confirms my impression that Wilson is at his best when he works with rigorously trained performers, whether actors, singers or dancers. The actors of the Comédie Française have a training comparable, in terms of precision and discipline, to that of French ballerina Sylvie Guillem, who performed in his *Le Martyre de Saint-Sébastien* at the Paris Opera in 1988. Their faith in formal perfection gave them the complete ease his productions require. At the same time, schooled to deliver texts for their meaning, they were able to capture the substance of the fables while shedding the constrictions of their word-centred training to meet Wilson's physical, movement-and-gesture demands.

LIGHT/COLOUR

'Without light, no space. Without space, no theatre' (Wilson in Teschke, 1999: 15). Wilson's variations on this axiom consistently stress the crucial importance of light. Thus: 'Light in my work is something special. To me, the most important element in theatre is light because it's the element that helps us to see and hear. Without light there's no space' (Enright, 1994: 20). And consider this: The theatre is 'architecture of space and light . . . . Without light there is no space. And time cannot exist without space. Space and time co-exist' (Wilson, 1997: 11–12). In this variation, Wilson refers to Giorgio Strehler, the only contemporary European director he appears to have acknowledged as his equal, and to Appia, whom he takes as his and Strehler's predecessor in matters of light.

Indeed, no one more than Appia passionately advocated the need 'to give to light its fullest power, and through it, integral plastic value to the actor and the scenic space' (Appia, 1993: 115). Light, Appia argued, must be active like the actor and in the latter's 'service' (ibid.: 114), ready to illuminate the three dimensions of his/her body in space rather than treat it in two dimensions, as if it were part of a backdrop. In its active capacity, light does not merely render something visible, but 'to be form-giving or plastic, light must exist in an atmosphere, a luminous atmosphere' (ibid.: 96). When this happens, light has tonal, vibratory, rhythmic and affective properties, just like music. Wilson's practice shows how deeply he concurs with all this, although he goes beyond Appia by having light do more than serve an actor: it becomes an actor in its own right. When an object is lit, says Wilson, 'and you cut out all the other lights . . . play occurs, and light assumes the function of an actor' (Grillet and Wilson, 1992: 8).

Enormous amounts of preparatory time are required to give light its proper status, calling for hundreds of cues when a production is lit. Wilson works closely with a lighting technician, naming the gels, fluorescence units, spots, combinations and intensities that might yield the palettes he needs. It is painstaking, fastidious labour, never more so than during rehearsals when the actors are lit, usually one by one. Days can go by with actors doing little more than stand about on the stage, light playing perpetually on them until it is fixed and recorded in the electronic lighting board. Light frequently seeks out parts of their body – head, face, hand, finger – which are isolated and illuminated for various effects. Wilson's hand in a cabaret-style sequence of *Hamlet*, for instance, is lit up for humour before the rest of his body appears. Elsewhere a spot picks out the back of his head for dramatic punch, or follows his face for satirical, meditative or tragic effect, depending on the given moment. Not one production goes by without Wilson dismembering the body, in some way, with light.

Whether bodies are fragmented or presented whole, they practically never cast shadows – a feat achieved in a translucent production like *Madama Butterfly* (1993) with some 450 lights at the sides and above the stage; the singers have to stay consistently in diagonal positions to keep the space shadowless. But Wilson has also devised techniques to kill shadows so that bodies look sculptured, and illuminated from within. He pays similarly close attention to the great walls, washes and panels of light in which he places his actors. Wilson usually works very methodically on one lighting aspect at a time, detail or big picture, gradually inventing a whole geometry in a panoply of shades whose changes alter space considerably. Many of his shades change in swift succession to build up rhythm and crescendos and diminuendos, some within one gamut of colour, most across several colour scales where the colours run into each other like musical notes. Wilson also has punctuation in light–colour: pauses, when a shade is held or tones merge; something like exclamation marks when lights black out suddenly, or when they swing radically from one colour to the next, or fire through the gels in staccato flashes. Active, performative light like this certainly has tempo, and builds up atmosphere, but its very action is dramatic. As such, it is a surrogate for what would normally be achieved by actors in psychological/ realistic theatre.

Wilson has increasingly explored the dramatic as well as narrative functions that he attributes to light, coloured light, especially. In *The Black Rider*, tubes of fluorescent light outline a large rifle that drops down from the flies and hangs in mid-air. Light draws the rifle to say that Wilhelm is going to the forest. It also indicates his attitude: the rifle is his 'light', his 'Holy Grail'. Garish purples, greens and reds frequently light references to the Devil, obsession and drug addiction, thus 'commenting' on them. An eerie pearly light announces Wilhelm's wedding where four Kätchen look-alikes in bridal white are grouped near the Devil, suggesting phantasms conjured up by the latter to confuse him (Figure 2.6).

In *Madama Butterfly* (1993), dramatic and narrative purposes are served by coloured light. Red and white, the colours of the Japanese flag, quickly pass on a cyclorama to suggest geographic location; the colour clue is reinforced by snatches of Japanese-style music in Puccini's score. Space and time are conveyed by subtleties of colour: pale blues slowly and softly merge into pinks and yellows to suggest the sky and mark the transition from night to dawn as Butterfly's vigil draws to an end. Her lover has failed to appear. That she waits only to orchestral music – there is neither singing nor action to help the story along – shows just how much the light has to tell, including from the character's point of view, which is not physically exteriorised by the soprano. The soprano looks calm, waiting with Butterfly in hope. The whole scene is a remarkable example of the principle of ellipsis discussed in the previous chapter regarding Wilson's historically dislocated productions. It also demonstrates in an especially fine way how he associates light with emotion and is able to elicit emotional responses from spectators accordingly.

Figure 2.6 *The Black Rider* (1990). Photograph by Clärchen Baus-Mattar, courtesy of Clärchen Baus-Mattar

Wilson increasingly explored the emotional function of coloured light. Perhaps the most dramatic examples come from *Woyzeck*, after Büchner's 1836 fragmented masterpiece. Woyzeck is a barber in the army, who is patronised by his sergeant, betrayed by his wife Marie, who sleeps with a Drum Major, and is a guinea pig for an army doctor's unscrupulous medical experiments, which destroy his mind. Crushed by social hierarchies, oppression, poverty and contempt, and driven by jealousy and despair, Woyzeck finally goes mad and murders Marie. That Woyzeck can do nothing but fail against overwhelming social and personal odds makes his the prototypical tragedy of the 'little man'. Wilson's dramaturgs, Wolfgang Wiens and Ann-Christin Rommen, heavily abridged Büchner's dialogue, replacing much of it with lyrics by Waits and Brennan. It is essential to note that these lyrics essentially operate like extrapolations, in another medium, of the underlying tone and mood of Büchner's text.

Wilson adopts a similarly extrapolative principle for his coloured light, painting the walls of the stage, a vast cyclorama and sides, alternately in milky white, sickly yellow, yellow-green, light green, deep green, scarlet and crimson. The floor is covered in complementary hues: chocolate brown to milky walls, for instance, or a deep green to yellow-green walls. In a scene where Woyzeck and Marie briefly embrace, the cyclorama is a glowing green which can acquire a specific resonance if spectators link it to a duet 'All the World is Green' sung by Waits for Marie and Woyzeck. Green, then, stands in a contiguous relation to their couple. It is, in a sense, 'their' colour. Spectators are told about their relationship in the past and its present, poignant, situation by the song's refrain: 'Pretend you owe me nothing/And all the world is green/Let's pretend we can bring back the old days again/And all the world is green.' Since these words make green the colour of happiness and harmony, they highlight the fact that Wilson extracts sense both from Büchner's drama and the text of his production, translating it into light—colour.

The green abruptly changes to a blazing red, radically altering the scene in accordance with Wilson's principle of juxtaposition and counterpoint. Red, throughout *Woyzeck*, is the colour of sex, passion, danger, violence, humiliation and jealousy, and spectators have time to associate the colour and these emotions during the performance. It stands, first and foremost, for Woyzeck so that 'his' emotions are concentrated in it when the cyclorama is flooded with red. In addition, red picks up its usual association in Western cultures with rage when Woyzeck murders Marie. The latter scene is first lit in soft greys and blues, and is built up with highly articulated movements reminiscent of a tango, but not specifically tango steps: feet are placed precisely, backs are arched, legs slide and so forth. Woyzeck and Marie dance to each other rather than with each other – there is no body contact between them – and their movements trace a circle, which, initially wide, narrows as Woyzeck prepares for the kill. So ambiguously do they step that it is difficult to say whether Marie is luring Woyzeck to his death, or whether he is leading her. But, for all its formality – everything in the dance is deliberate, contoured – the actors are focused so intensely on it that, irrespective of their cold appearance, they fill the space with their intensity. Meanwhile, the light works subliminally on the spectators' emotions, helping them 'to see' in the broader sense of 'apprehend' and 'feel' also meant by Wilson, as cited earlier.

The light enveloping Woyzeck and Marie changes colour increasingly rapidly as their dance progresses: Wilson's trademark luminous blue along with translucent white, yellow and green and their blends; the green of 'All the World is Green' flashes past, and a murky brown settles momentarily before it cedes to another, startling red. This turmoil of hot and cold colours has affective qualities to the extent that they play on the spectators' feelings but, equally, because they can be taken to be the visual correlative of the characters' inward terrors. Similarly, these very colours externalise the situation of conflict between them.

While light tells the spectator what is happening, another light begins to form a huge lower half of a circle on the cyclorama and slowly deepens, going from red to brown to near black. As the shape appears to pulsate and expand – a pure optical illusion – the walls turn scarlet and then go through a range of tones of deep red. Towards the end of this metamorphosis, a fine curve of brilliant red tinges the bottom rim of the near-black half-circle, which hangs, heavily (the illusion of weight created by the size and darkness of the shape) and as if suspended, just above the floor. By the time this happens, Marie is on her back on the floor in a pose, one arm lifted and her knees bent. Woyzeck is beside her, leaning forward with an exquisitely beautiful knife in his hand whose gleaming triangular-shaped blade is poised just above Marie's neck. That suspended moment in the silent dance is how Woyzeck 'kills' her (Figure 2.7).

Figure 2.7 *Woyzeck* (2000). Photograph by Erik Hansen-Hansen, courtesy of Hansen-Hansen.com

Numerous associations would be appropriate for this tremendous murder scene, but perhaps the most powerful of them would be that of the sun. It could be an eclipse of the sun, or an apocalyptic sign, or the black sun of melancholia and madness, as figured in countless European paintings and poems; and it is madness that overwhelms Woyzeck in Büchner's play. Nevertheless, no matter how the threatening, menacing half-circle is perceived, it looks as if it is about to crush Marie. In this ominous light, she also ends her difficult existence. 'I do everything with light', claims Wilson (Wilson, 1997: 12), and reiterates:

> lighting determines everything else: it works with the music or confronts it, makes things transparent or lays out zones, orders movement, breaks up the text and structures the set. It is anything but an extra, it structures and assembles and, consequently, it drives the text and the music. And not the other way round.
>
> (Wilson, 2005: 51)

We can see from *Woyzeck* exactly what he means.

TEXT

Woyzeck is not Büchner's play set to music, but an extrapolation from Büchner's concerns. Thus its songs go to the heart of Büchner's universe without being *in* that universe, immersion of some kind being the usual expectation of theatre working closely on texts. Songs titled 'Misery is The River of the World' and 'God's Away on Business' paraphrase Woyzeck's account of a society without justice, run by money, power and sex. In such a society, God – cast by Waits as a heartless capitalist – is indeed away on business. Bittersweet songs ('My Coney Island Girl') or cynically brutal ones ('Everything Goes to Hell') transfer the Woyzeck–Marie story into another time and idiom.

Wilson's indirect take on Buchner's text has to do with his early rejection of a theatre that gives first priority to texts. His approach is relational, making all the components of a production equally important, and this is a safeguard against a theatre that 'privileges confrontation and absorption too much' (Friedl, 1982: 56). Second, he believes that language is inadequate: 'We cannot express the totality of what we feel with words, it's too complex' (ibid.). Third, his mistrust of semantics (inseparable, of course, from language) is tied up with his desire to keep meanings open: there cannot be one meaning, only numerous 'interpretative possibilities' (Eco, 1993: 90). Wilson's notion of 'possibilities' undergirds his rejection of 'interpretation', which he (mis)interprets to mean something like 'only one way' (as transpires from Umberto Eco's interview with him, as cited earlier in this chapter; ibid.: 89–91). Fourth, Wilson's rejection of the very idea that any work can be 'understood' is behind his disclaimer to 'understand' texts:

> The works are larger than the man.... I don't think that Shakespeare understood what he wrote. It's something that one can think about and reflect on, but not completely understand.... It is not possible to fully comprehend *King Lear*.
>
> (Ibid.: 90)

Fifth, Wilson believes that a 'great work' can neither be fully understood (to claim to do otherwise is to '*fix* an interpretation' and thus 'limit or narrow the work'; Enright, 1994: 17), nor provide him with definite answers. His task in the theatre is 'to ask questions . . . . If you know why you are doing something then there's no need to do it' (ibid.).

It is clear from the foregoing that, for Wilson, texts should be perceived as open-ended and redolent with multiple meanings. The 1990s were a turning point, bringing him closer to this idea of texts then ever before, and *Hamlet* may well have been a decisive moment because Wilson performed all the parts himself. Even as a non-interpretative actor, he would have had to battle with the 'possibilities' of words in order to place them in relation to his other stage elements. Indeed, Ann-Christin Rommen confirms that, when rehearsing, he ceaselessly asked what Shakespeare's words 'meant', and worried over them till he 'got' them (7 February 2005). And Wilson's fastidious work on the text would also have adhered to his principle of 'filling' forms with 'interior reflection'. But he was no longer imparting this principle from the outside to actors. *He* was now the actor and his forms had to be full of reverberations coming from *him*. It could be argued that, irrespective of Wilson's open-ended approach, it was his attention to textual detail that led him to focus exclusively on Hamlet's inner state of being. This made his production, thematically speaking, a *Hamlet* practically like no other except that of Brook (2000), and, to a lesser extent, of Robert Lepage as *Elsinore* (1995–97). Furthermore, his 'interior reflection' on Hamlet's words is such that they have a personal ring, as no other piece performed by him previously.

Hamlet was conceived as a solo in what ultimately looks like a performance piece or an installation – the case also of *Orlando*. This quality suffuses most of Wilson's drama productions not excluding those that have epic scope, like *Dream Play* and *Peer Gynt*. It throws into relief their story lines, as traced by Wilson in his visual books; and he makes sure that these lines are never lost, even when they appear anything but linear to the eye and ear. *Dream Play*, for instance, is a visual collage, but, where story-telling is concerned, it actually does follow Strindberg's text to the end, and does so regardless of the numerous cuts made to the text.

On the other hand, the story-telling of *Peer Gynt* is visibly more sequential. Wilson's script is concise, for to cover Ibsen's text entirely would have meant a nine-hour production instead of four. Nevertheless, it retains Ibsen's core dialogue and noticeably retains the philosophical, ethical and social reflections fundamental to Act V, where an old Peer returns home to Norway. It was evident during rehearsals of this Act how Wilson trusted Sverre Bentzen, the third 'Peer', to seek out the meanings of the words as they meant to *him* in play. What Wilson did was to provide cues: 'get through the words' so that they are 'lighter';

'stretch your text a little more' so that it has 'more tension'; 'make it slower' so that it sounds less 'naturalistic' and more 'formal', and similarly indicative directions (10 February 2005). Wilson's directions, then, did anything but offer character or other interpretations of any kind; and he wisely desisted from interfering in the semantics of a foreign language that he neither speaks nor understands. That, precisely, was the job of his dramaturg.

IMAGE (TEXT)

Everything in Wilson's work is a matter of images – visual, sonic, kinetic – as detailed in the preceding pages. It suffices now to observe how his images are 'textual' in the sense that they can become crystallisations, in one imagistic swoop, of an aspect or part of a text, and even of a whole text. Take the example of Woyzeck who repeatedly runs on the spot at a very fast pace or, occasionally, in a full circle around the stage with the look and movements of an automaton: knees very high, arms bent in parallel, hands and fingers stretched forward, body rigid, and white, mask-like face leaning forward. Woyzeck's running seems disconnected, and can stay that way in the spectator's mind. On the other hand, it can be seen to be Wilson's imagistic rendition of a meaning constructed in Büchner's text, namely, that poor Woyzeck gets nowhere in life.

A similar image of running occurs in Act II of *Peer Gynt*. In Ibsen's dialogue, Peer and the trolls refer to the bells that start ringing and which will save Peer from them. Wilson keeps these lines to a minimum, and 'ends' the scene with a blackout in which is heard, almost immediately, a loud amplified clip-clop sound going around the auditorium, now zooming out, now zooming in. The nature of this sound is not clear until the first 'Peer', Henrik Rafaelsen, appears running in a circle on the stage. What, at first, is a slender, flat silver ring soon becomes a thick 'ring of steam', as Wilson calls it in his visual book (Act II, scene vii). The billowing steam in the blue–black space represents the Great Boyg, and Rafaelsen keeps running quickly and lightly to the sound, which is still amplified, but now closer, as if coming from the stage. This merger of the end of one scene with the whole of another, all without words, certainly tells us that Peer has been running away from the trolls in the mountains, only to run away again from the Boyg. However, as is evident at a deeper textual level of Ibsen's play, Peer spends his entire life running away from something, someone and his 'self'; and it is exactly this web of meanings that Wilson seizes imagistically. Ibsen's text is elided, but caught.

SILENCE, SOUND, MUSIC

The silent operas were instrumental in Wilson's development, as we have already noted. Later, he stressed that silence and sound were not alternate but continuous:

> If you're speaking a line, especially in a text as fragmented as this one [*Golden Windows*], the silence is a continuation of the sound.... Whether you're speaking or not speaking, it's the same thing. John Cage says there's no such thing as silence.... When you stop speaking, you're still aware of sound. It's one continuous movement. It's not stop and start.
>
> (Letzler Cole, 1992: 150)

The principle of continuity evoked by Wilson goes well beyond how lines or whole sections of a text are delivered. It structurally governs the relation between non-spoken pieces like Act II, scene vii of *Peer Gynt* discussed earlier and the otherwise verbal textures into which Wilson 'inserts' them. Take, as another kind of example, the fable 'The Wind and the Reed' which is the only one of the La Fontaine selection that he renders without words. Here silence and the whistling wind are 'one continuous movement'. The wind's power is not so much shown aurally as visually by a 'mighty' oak, pictured as a long, dark shape bending closer and closer to the ground. Meanwhile, the thin but resilient reed bends with the wind, but unlike the oak, is not torn down by its force. The presence of this sole 'silent' fable among others spoken or vocally articulated in some other way by their characters seems to throw into relief the fact that the flow of the whole work is uninterrupted. Several fables that have silences of various length between sound, verbal or not, give the same impression. The sonorities of language are exploited to the full (a practice begun with *A Letter for Queen Victoria*) and their very reverberations accentuate the silences – something Wilson never tires of doing in his entire *oeuvre*.

Wordless sound can be a prelude to a scene, as is typical of opera. Act V of *Peer Gynt* begins with crashing waves and a high wind coming from behind the auditorium, thrown into darkness. It is gradually overlaid by snatches of music and, in counterpoint, by an amplified voice reciting a scientific treatise completely unrelated to Ibsen's text. This interlude lasts for about four minutes while a major scene change takes place behind a black curtain, which is not visible, in any case, in the blackout. It is a ploy for technical reasons, but also serves Wilson's aim for continuity between the 'prelude' and the scene 'proper'.

The scene is preceded by a huge crash of waves. The lights go up on three white ropes rising to the flies. These ropes, a ladder with a human figure at the top, and three men in oilskins and rubber boots, all of whom sway very slightly – the hands of one mime, almost imperceptibly, the steering of a wheel – are the 'ship' on which Peer returns home (Figure 2.8). The sound of creaking wood and a gentle, musical whistling so different from the blowing wind accompany the men's movements. A few more minutes pass before this marvellous tableau of sound and sight breaks into dialogue whose content, while important, as in Ibsen's text, is not overshadowed by the sonic qualities and musicality of the words. Wilson's score for this scene combines what could be called the poetry of words, natural sounds, invented sounds and musical notes. Once again, although especially transparent in *Peer Gynt*, it is representative of how such scores operate in all Wilson productions.

All of Wilson's scores weave silence in, to whatever degree, and are generally tissues of varied rhythms, tempi, tones, timbres, inflections, frequencies, pitches and volume. The language of a given production, frequently not English, contributes its own, particular gamut of tones, timbres, and so forth. Not being a speaker of foreign languages, Wilson relies on these features of language as well as on its physicality and materiality. The physical properties of language are rendered by how the actors utter not only with their mouths (plucking words out, for example), but through their bodies, which they use as a kind of resonance chamber for amplifying sound or hollowing it out, among other things. This is exactly what inspired him to have a text in *The Meek Girl* recited in three different languages, French, German and English, the physicality of the one all the more palpable for its counterpoint with the next. *Peer Gynt*, at the behest of Det Norske Teatret, is performed in New Norwegian, a kind of 'national' language made from the dialects of Norway that is understood by all in the country but is not actually its spoken language. Jon Fosse, the well-known playwright, who translated Ibsen's Norwegian to this constructed tongue advised the dramaturg so that the body and the shape of the sounds could be fully realised on the stage.

Sound exploration of this kind evolves in rehearsals, where Wilson will ask this or that actor to sing a text, whisper it softly or loudly, laugh it or

Figure 2.8 *Peer Gynt* (2005). Photograph by Lesley Leslie-Spinks, courtesy of Lesley Leslie-Spinks

laugh into it, use a tenor rather than a base voice, vary the register of the voice, or pitch it beyond its natural spoken or sung range, and more still. Sometimes he will ask an actor to retain traces of the vocal quality he or she had found while experimenting, but not actually make that sound as such. This permits modulation and shading, and encourages actors to seek and hold emotion in their voice. One of his signatures is what Wilson calls the 'silent scream', probably thinking of the Norwegian painter Edvard Munch, famous for his *The Silent Scream* canvases. Actors across his productions 'freeze' quick, silent screams. These screams are visual simulations whose counterparts are the animal- and/or human-like screams, cries, howls, growls and screeches scattered in them all. Whichever production serves as an example, it is the *balance* between the sounds, and between sound and sight, that determines Wilson's choice and combination.

Sound is always projected through microphones discretely attached to the actors, which allow it to function like a mask. Wilson's technique supports his claim that his 'entire stage is a mask' (Fuchs, 1986: 102); like the Greek stage peopled by masked actors, its images are different from what is heard (ibid.). We could add that this discrepancy between sight and sound generates distance, and distance, we have seen again and again, is a fundamental Wilson principle. Wilson remarks: 'That's one reason I use microphones – to create a distance between the sound and the image' (ibid.).

However, he cannot use microphones in anything like the same way in opera where the power of the singing voice is expected to fill the theatre, and where any significant departure from this norm would threaten the singers' integrity. In fact, Wilson recognises that the retention of emotion in the voice to which he aspires in the theatre is indispensable for opera. He does not always manage to carry it off, but his four productions of Wagner's *Ring*, possibly the most musically invasive work of the entire operatic repertoire and one that makes the greatest demands on the voice, are distinguished by how voices have full control over emotions. The absolute minimalism of Wilson's stage is designed to give these voices the free space they need.

BODY/MOVEMENT

So much has been said during the course of this book about the body and movement that further detail is not necessary. However, an additional point of principle requires attention, and it has to do with a quality of body-movement that can only be called 'grotesque'. This quality appears most noticeably in Wilson's work with and after *The Black Rider*. It is redolent in all his rock-folk music theatre, not least *Woyzeck*, and even seeps through such refined works as *Les Fables*.

The term, as applicable to Wilson, is best served by Meyerhold's idea of the 'grotesque', which can be summed up, in my words, as something unexpected and surprising that makes whatever is everyday and familiar appear strange; something exaggerated and theatricalised that is open to sardonic reflection; something that, by its sharp, even strident edge, makes an apparently purely formal feature an instrument of moral and social criticism (Meyerhold, 1998: 137–42). Take *Woyzeck* where 'grotesque' in this composite sense is evident in the dance-like phrases of the characters who deride Woyzeck (his Captain, his doctors, the Drum Major), all of them de-authenticated and made to look strange by being overdone. Sudden changes in their highly theatrical movements, say, from gallantry to thuggishness, obliges spectators to see the incipient critique in these movements. The whole of *The Black Rider* is arguably in a grotesque mode with the exception, perhaps, that it does not altogether fulfil Meyerhold's criterion of social critique.

Furthermore, the goal of plastic beauty, or what Meyerhold calls the 'decorative task', is indispensable to this conception of the grotesque. As Meyerhold puts it:

> The art of the grotesque is based on the conflict between form and content. The grotesque aims to subordinate psychologism to a decorative task. That is why in every theatre which has been dominated by the grotesque the aspect of design in its widest sense has been so important (for example the Japanese theatre). Not only the settings, the architecture of the stage, and the theatre itself are decorative, but also the mime, movements, gestures and poses of the actors. Through being decorative they become expressive. For this reason the technique of the grotesque contains elements of the dance; only with the help of the dance is it possible to subordinate grotesque conceptions to a decorative task.

(Ibid.: 141)

Let us take *Woyzeck* again in which is to be found every element cited by Meyerhold, including the subordination of 'psychologism to a decorative task' that motivates the grotesque. Wilson subordinates what would otherwise be Woyzeck's psychological make-up to the 'decorative task' of light. Thus, light, which is fundamental to Wilson's 'design in its widest sense', becomes expressive of Woyzeck's psychological state. Similarly, dance-like movement – also part of design – is 'expressive' in so far as it speaks for the characters on the stage in ways that their words do not. The 'tango' murder scene does this eloquently. When emphasis is placed on the notion of stylised movement inherent in Meyerhold's concept of the 'grotesque' – witness his reference to Japanese theatre – this concept reveals its relevance for Wilson's theatre work as a whole.

COSTUMES

Costumes, designed by others, work within Wilson's aesthetic and change with it. His silent operas are based on his principle of counterpoint – unadorned everyday dress, for the most part, against touches of formal wear like Victorian gowns, parasols, ties and tails. In the productions going from *Freud* to *Edison*, sartorial references are made to the people named in their titles, but are far from costume portraits in a realistic manner. Similarly, historically recognisable details of dress in *the CIVIL warS*, *Orlando*, *Hamlet* and *The Winter's Tale*, among others, connote rather than denote a historical period. Thus, for the last three productions cited, a glove, a jacket and a gown suggest Elizabethan times. Such allusions are especially tantalising in *The Winter's Tale* because they are relatively few in the rich costume fantasia that Jacques Reynaud clearly loves to create.

The more elaborate Wilson's work becomes visually through light–colour and gesture, the more fanciful and even sometimes out-landish are its costumes, all of which distance those who wear them in another variant of the 'grotesque'. *The Black Rider*, for instance (costumes by Frida Parmeggiani, frequently his costume designer for opera), is a box of grotesque tricks, its wardrobe patterned on a mixture of vampire movies and *The Wizard of Oz* and *Star Wars*. There are such details as fangs (to go with Wilhelm's Old Uncle's Dracula cape), a rope tail (to go with the Devil's long coat) and vivid green socks (to go with Wilhelm's too-short, *Oz*-style trousers). All smile at the stereotypes that they appropriate in such a blatantly theatricalised way. *Woyzeck*, in another example (costumes by Reynaud), delights in butch red-leather outfits for the Drum Major and very chic, but highly unreal stiff frocks cut in panels with jagged hems for Marie. Her dress could be said to mirror, by its effect, the mannequin-actor who is in the role, and is related both to Meyerhold's 'design' actor and Craig's 'puppet' actor. Marie's clothes, moreover, echo the geometry of the lopsided distorted houses and walls that appears on screens as Woyzeck's madness progresses (Figure 2.9).

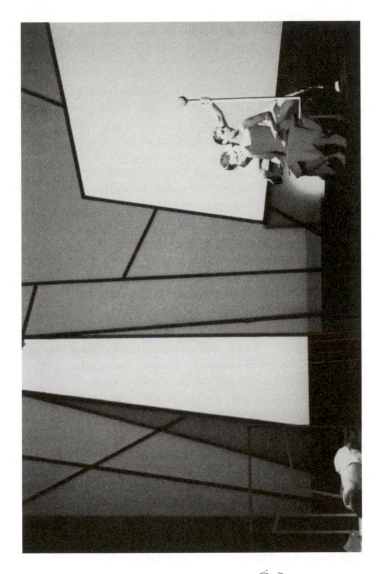

Figure 2.9
Woyzeck (2000).
Photograph by
Erik Hansen-
Hansen,
courtesy
of Hansen-
Hansen.com

At times, couturier extremes compensate for what appears to be insecure or unresolved from a dramaturgical point of view, as occurs in *The Winter's Tale*. Faced with the enigma of Act IV of the play – why is so much room given here to Autolycus, the Clown and clowning in general? – Wilson goes with the flow and allows these characters and their antics to govern Act IV of his production. His decision results in a pronounced gestural and visual semiotics. Autolycus and the Clown are a madcap pair dressed in zany garments that are too short or too tight and whose colours clash violently. The actor in the role of Autolycus sports bright yellow, plastic shoes that show-off his fancy footwork (Figure 2.10). All in all, the Act shows clowning pushed to the extreme and, although finally tedious, it arguably helps to reinforce the production's emphasis on the improbable, which corresponds to the imaginary, 'tale' dimension of Shakespeare's text.

Garments in Wilson's productions are frequently uncomfortable to wear, yet the actors have to move lightly in them. When rehearsing *The Black Rider* in London, Wilson pointed out to the cast that their costumes were made of heavy material, much of it paper and felt, which did not 'breathe, and the lights are hot' (6 May 2004). He consequently urged the actors to be 'calm and concentrated' and listen to each other so as 'to be one entity'. But these costumes, like most used by Wilson, have what couturiers call 'body', which is normally achieved through the type of fabric used, its cut, and its upholstery of bones, wires, hoops and related support. This contributes to the sculptured look of his actors and can also suggest that they are wearing armour or some other kind of protective shield, thereby reinforcing the distance their very being is meant to project.

When costumes flow, they extend the bodyline of the actor and elongate movement as well. For example, the extremely long train of the gown worn by Childs in *La Maladie de la mort is* intrinsic to her movement, determining its form and duration. Erda, the Earth Goddess of the *Ring* tetralogy, exits upwards on a raked stage while the endless train of her silk gown follows her, creating the imperious but mysterious movement so necessary for this opera. The costumes of Wilson's work during and after the 1990s are generally sensuous and splendid, and light plays on them to enhance their allure. They are not clothes, but poetry.

OBJECTS

Objects, though usually few, are employed to great effect to highlight the architecture and arrangement of productions, and to mark out time

Figure 2.10 *The Winter's Tale* (2005). Photograph by Lesley Leslie-Spinks, courtesy of Lesley Leslie-Spinks

and space, like the descending chair in *Freud*. Objects might denote or complete an action, as occurs when a frog holds a glass to its lips in *Deafman Glance*. They can be functional – witness the chairs that, here and there in Wilson's *oeuvre*, are used for sitting, although they are necessary design elements. They can also extend costumes, like the armour plate wings that drop from the flies for Isabelle Huppert and offset her sculptured demeanour (Figure 2.11).

Frequently, objects are simply playful, like the toys on display in the opening of *The Black Rider*. Or else they are used playfully for narrative purposes. In Act III of *Peer Gynt*, for example, a tiny ship appears on the cyclorama at the back of the stage, its size indicating that it is sailing away on the horizon. Ibsen's play tells us that the ship was stolen from Peer who, in the preceding scene, bragged about his commercial exploits to the men about to rob him. Wilson's object also shows what happens after Peer's ship was stolen: the tiny object suddenly explodes in mid-sea. This playfulness is also humorous. A similar combination of narrative placing and fun recurs when several minuscule palm trees unexpectedly dot the cyclorama at the beginning of Act IV to locate the desert. How Wilson began to use objects in multiple ways is an integral part of the following discussion of *Einstein on the Beach*.

Figure 2.11 *Orlando* (1993). Photograph by Abisag Tüllman

3

EINSTEIN ON THE BEACH

ITINERARY AND RECEPTION

The show was sold out long before *Einstein on the Beach* was premiered at the Avignon Festival in 1976 and received a thunderous standing ovation. The press was equally enthusiastic. *Le Monde*, the newspaper 'for intellectuals', declared that Wilson 'had lived up, once again, to his legend' (28 July 1976). *Le Figaro*, the bastion of conservative opinion, observed that the production's slowed-down pace and minute shifts of movement took spectators out of their normal world into a 'universe beyond the laws of natural physics'; the whole was a 'fascinating experience' (27 July 1976). All reviews recalled the sensation caused by *Deafman Glance* five years earlier so as to claim that *Einstein*, a different kind of work, was just as revolutionary. Criticism came only from *L'Aurore*: the production was 'fantastically imaginative', but Wilson's art led to an impasse, its 'obsessive stuttering and eternal repetition' making it look like 'a lesson for the re-education of the mentally disabled, a therapy for depression, a cure for insomniacs or a psycho-motor nightmare' (*L'Aurore*, 28 July 1976). This sting in the tail of praise could be compared to a 'down' after the 'high' induced by *Einstein*'s visual, sonic and body rhythms, which appeared obsessive, like actions under the influence of narcotics, and lasted four hours and 40 minutes without an intermission.

The production embarked on its six-country European tour, which included the hugely prestigious Autumn Festival in Paris, a showcase for avant-garde work. Some 30 performances later, all generating immense excitement, *Einstein* returned to New York where it had been constructed and rehearsed thanks to the sponsorship referred to of the French Ministry of Culture; most probably the work would have never seen the light of day without this financial and moral support. International funding had also come from the Venice Biennale, and the sets were made in Milan to facilitate their transport to the production's opening in Avignon. *Einstein* was performed in New York at the Metropolitan Opera, although not in the Metropolitan's regular programme but during its 'dark' nights on two consecutive Sundays. The engagement was arranged with the help of Jerome Robbins who, we saw, had performed briefly in Wilson's *Freud*, but was renowned for his choreography of *West Side Story*. He had also accrued considerable prestige from fine choreographies for the New York City Ballet. Robbins had telephoned from Paris, where he had just seen *Einstein*, insisting that someone from the Metropolitan should fly over to see it. This was done, and the show was signed up for the house. Wilson stresses that timing is of the essence for his compositions, but, clearly, it also applies to their successful dissemination.

The Metropolitan has 4,000 seats and, if standing room is counted, holds 4,500 people. Composer Philip Glass states how worried he had been that 'the Met would be half empty' (Glass, 1988: 52) – a fear not unfounded given that the Metropolitan was a most unlikely venue for this unconventional opera. 'Opera' was the term on which Wilson had insisted, even though Glass had originally preferred to think of it as 'music-theatre' (Shyer, 1989: 220). Glass notes with a touch of humour that, although Wilson called all his pieces 'opera', 'maybe he thought that with me he could finally do a real one' (ibid.).

There was no need for concern. *Einstein*'s triumph in Europe had been registered in America and the house was full to the rafters on both Sundays. This was a far cry from the 'audience totalling barely two dozen people' for the performance of *A Letter for Queen Victoria* which the reviewer Robert T. Jones had attended at a Broadway theatre for musicals, just two years before (Jones in Glass, 1988: viii). According to Glass, 'some in the audience' for *Einstein* 'had mistakenly thought that an evening at the Met would hold to a more traditional line', although most spectators expected 'something new and unusual' (ibid.: 53);

and if numbers of them 'stormed out after the first half-hour or so', the entire house was up on its feet at the end of the performance in a storm of calls and applause. The Metropolitan was no gift, however, despite the production's resounding success. Glass and Wilson were left nearly $150,000 in debt (Shyer, 1989: 229). The deficit took years to pay off, but the experience, felt with a keen sense of responsibility by Wilson, steeled him for the numerous difficult negotiations over money in which his work was always to be involved in the future, *the CIVIL warS* being a prime example, as we saw in the first chapter.

The critical reception in New York was just as robust as that of the public. Clive Barnes from the *New York Times* remarked that the 'avant-garde always runs the risk of the ridiculous, the peril of the irrelevant', but 'Robert Wilson is the exception' (23 November 1976). The figure of Einstein, he suggested, was Wilson and Glass's symbol of 'the affinity between mathematics and beauty . . . . The mind that caught the limitless theory of the expanding universe also sparked the atomic bomb.' But, whether the work actually meant this was not, he believed, of any importance:

> You are either interested by its ritualistic pictures, its verbal and musical convolutions and its languorous sense of fantasy, or you are not. You then are bored rather than sedated, annoyed rather than excited, insulted rather than intrigued . . . . You will never forget it, even if you hate it. Which is a most rare attribute to a work of art. Nowadays.

> (Ibid.)

Mel Gussow, also of the *New York Times*, described the production as a 'science-fiction opera-play' and stressed its 'suspension of traditional theatrical expectation', its 'strict structural form, co-ordinated through theatre, music, dance and design' and its 'insistent, ear-piercing' score which was 'ultimately as hypnotic as the play itself' (28 November 1976). All of it had 'an eerie, other-worldly quality that occasionally makes us feel that we are on Mars rather than at the Met' (ibid.). Gussow's way of identifying *Einstein* with a cluster of nouns ('science fiction', 'opera', 'play') reminds us of how radically Wilson's practice had called into question the very idea of generic categories, obliging commentators to fall back on composite names for his pieces, or on such new ones as 'hybrids' and 'crossovers' (which are, of course, new categories). Wilson maintained from the start – and continued to say it – that he was not interested in categorisation: his was simply a different way of seeing things.

The memory of *Einstein on the Beach* as weird and wonderful was strong enough to inspire its revival in 1984 for the cutting-edge Next Wave Festival at the Brooklyn Academy of Music (BAM). The *New York Times* ran an article with the heading 'The Avant-Garde Is Big Box Office' and pointed out that *Einstein* would be a 'surefire hit . . . having already sold out its run of 12 performances in the Academy's 2,100-seat opera house' (16 December 1984). The reviewers confirmed the prognosis. John Rockwell, for example, who had seen *Einstein* in Avignon, at which time he had called it an 'astonishing modern-day mystery play' (*New York Times*, 1 August 1976), now announced that the revival was even better than the original and, 'constantly involving and almost religiously moving', it would provide for those who were as affected as he was 'experiences to cherish for a lifetime' (*New York Times*, 17 December 1984). For Rockwell, the question of the work's resistance to meaning, and whether this mattered, did not arise at all as it had done for his colleague Barnes eight years before. He was sure of its subject matter:

> Above all, *Einstein* is about light: its beauty, its relation to energy and power, and ultimately its mystical connection to love (from the final speech: 'you are the light of my life, my sun, moon and stars').
>
> (Ibid.)

Amidst the general hubbub, the normally reticent Wilson insinuated that he would have liked Americans to discover *Death Destruction and Detroit*, which 'is so dense, so rich, so complicated. *Einstein* is from another period – very static, and flat, using compressed space, very two-dimensional' (cited in the *New York Times*, 2 December 1984). It is relevant to remember here the bitter disappointment Wilson had felt in March 1984 when the Los Angeles Olympic Arts Festival cancelled his *CIVIL warS* due to lack of funds. Pleased as he was that New York had managed to finance *Einstein* for the Next Wave Festival, he must have been smarting at the thought that his most recent and most ambitious project had been so ignominiously treated in his own country. *Einstein* turned out to be a commercial success, doubling by itself alone the festival's whole takings in the previous year. After the event, its artistic success was also indisputable. That this 'legendary spectacle brought back from mythic limbo' had 'moved many to exhilaration and tears', as it had done in 1976, was taken to be 'a tribute to the truly visionary power of this performance masterwork' (Howell, 1985: 90).

The 1984 revival was by no means a straight reproduction, even though it had kept the original's structure and 'way-out' feel, along with many of its performance particulars. The original dervish-like dances by Andrew de Groat, which I remember as gripping in 1976, regardless of the 'friendly, unassuming, *faux-naif* air about them' (Howell, 1985: 90), were performed by the team of multi-tasked singer-actor-dancers who, primarily for reasons of costs, had handled everything in the 1976 version, except the instruments. The Philip Glass Ensemble played these. Re-choreographed by Lucinda Childs, the opera's two dance sections were still 20 minutes long. However, now more virtuosic and precise than before, they required trained dancers, whom Childs provided from her own dance company. The rhythms of Childs's new choreography were also sharper, and her re-iterative, accentuated steps enhanced the intricacies of Glass's music, highlighting the fact that the music and Wilson's staging were meant to run in parallel rather than to interpret each other.

The stage performers had changed, as well. Only the principal per-formers Lucinda Childs and Sheryl Sutton had remained, together with the 77-year old Samuel Johnson, who concludes the production with the panegyric on love cited earlier ('you are the light of my life'). The fourth remaining performer was Wilson himself who, shortly before Johnson's final speech, dances a speedy solo torch dance, lights flashing in the semi-darkness. What *Einstein* had lost in artisanal roughness, which was appealing in 1976, it had gained in professionalism and power, qualities closer to the temper of 1984. Glass has been quoted as saying half-jokingly that 'this production is what we would have done in 1976 if we had known what we were doing' (cited in Howell, 1985: 90). This toned-up and streamlined *Einstein* was revived in 1992. It was still a knockout for audiences, and still gave rise to such grandiloquence from critics as 'one of the *Zeitgeist*-defining artistic creations' [of the twentieth century] (*Washington Post*, 21 November 1992).

Why had *Einstein* 'withstood the test of time' once again, eight years later in 1992, as Rockwell had already claimed it had done in 1984, eight years after its first appearance in 1976 (*New York Times*, 17 December 1984)? Why did it still have such impact? Part of the answer might lie in Glass's observation in 1993 that *Einstein on the Beach* struck him as being more radical in the present than in 1976: the 1970s was a period of experimentation but, since then, the theatre in America had become 'much more conventional' (cited in Holmberg, 1996: 21). In a climate dominated by the box office, 'young audiences . . . have no idea you could get away with making theatre in such a non-traditional way' (ibid.). He and Wilson had thought 'about aesthetics, not success', and not at all about whether the production would go anywhere else after they had finished it (ibid.).

Well, concentration on *Einstein*'s aesthetics *did* result in touring, even in the longer term. After its 1992 revival, *Einstein* went for the first time to Barcelona, Melbourne and Tokyo, among other cities, and was performed again at BAM and the Autumn Festival in Paris. The analytical discussion to follow will concern this 1984/1992 version and will open up a work described by another critic as 'not always easy or intelligible' (Banes, 1998: 25).

EINSTEIN ON THE BEACH: A LANDMARK

Einstein on the Beach is of great importance for several reasons:

- It is a milestone in the history of twentieth-century performance.
- It is a cultural icon in so far as it crystallises and transcends the experimental trends of all the arts across the board during the 1960s and 1970s in the United States.
- It is one of the first, major examples of late twentieth-century internationalism in the theatre and of what today is called globalisation, expressed in how it was financed, distributed and sustained over time.
- It is a salient example of how a production can stir up strong, contradictory passions whose potency reflects its social significance and confirms its artistic stature.

Where Wilson's body of work is specifically concerned:

- It is a turning point in Wilson's artistic development, being his first piece of music theatre and leading him to make numerous music theatre productions in the broadest sense of the term, which includes grand opera.
- It is a landmark, by its comprehensive nature, in Wilson's crisscross journey over the boundaries that traditionally define artistic genres and separate 'high' and 'popular' culture.

- Its extensive dance sequences make it uniquely dance-like, and foreshadow the pervasive role played by dance movement in Wilson's subsequent works.
- Its apparently paradoxical status as both an avant-garde and a main stage piece defines the direction Wilson's career was to take – a whiz-kid innovator working in established institutions across the world.

STRUCTURE AND FORM

What *is* this work that is, at once, a beginning and a major achievement, and seminal as well as influential, but somehow unique, out there on its own? How is it made intelligible when spectators, in the process of watching it, are absorbed most of all by its mystery?

Wilson explains that he always starts with a title and then determines the structure and duration of the proposed work (Huppert, 1994: 65). He then fills this 'architecture' (Wilson's term) with content. His architectural approach, together with his sense of organisation and exactitude, suited Glass's way of writing music, and the two men went about their respective tasks, although not as fully independently of each other as Cunningham and Cage. Wilson, for instance, would suggest images for Glass to think about for the music, and it was he who asked for an aria and 'that there should be singing throughout the piece' (Glass in Shyer, 1989: 220). Arias, of course, are an opera convention, but the one Glass composed for a soprano was on a few modulated notes without words, a decision totally in keeping with his 'minimalist', seemingly repetitive, but in fact perpetually changing score. Glass, in any case, was more than capable of delivering the goods. He was a highly educated, published and performed composer who led an established music ensemble. Moreover, he had a wealth of theatre experience behind him having collaborated since the 1960s with Mabou Mines, a group pioneering collective improvisation and devising.

The idea of Einstein for an opera came from Wilson's desire to work around a popular hero about whom everyone knew something. His title was inspired by a postcard of the scientist by the seashore, but the opera is no more biographical than any of Wilson's other productions supposedly 'about' individuals (*The Life and Times of Joseph Stalin*, *Edison* and so on, discussed earlier in this book). Although random, the title serves as a reference for images and actions that may be associated with Einstein. There are clocks, gyroscopes, small paper aeroplanes and a toy-like spaceship, as well as a contraption the size of the stage whose lights sizzle like fireworks and suggest a spaceship out of hell or a blockbuster movie. There is an eclipse of the moon and a picture of a nuclear explosion. A man repeatedly writes into space what appears to be Einstein's formula $E = mc^2$. These allusions are scattered across the production, only capable of being brought together in the spectator's mind afterwards. They refer, of course, if only tangentially, to Einstein's theory of relativity which concerns energy, light, mass, motion, speed, time and space; and all these are enacted or embodied in some way – speed of dance or moving beam of light – so as to suggest that they are the very subject of the myriad of images and sounds swirling from the stage and the orchestra pit. *Einstein on the Beach* could be said to be, in a piecemeal but, nevertheless, very tangible way, Wilson's meditation on space and time. Space and time, we have seen, are the fundamental subjects of his work as a whole.

Wilson and Glass decided that *Einstein* would be four hours long and have four acts and five connecting interludes that Wilson calls 'Knee Plays' (because they are like the joints of the human body). One Knee Play would open the work and one would close it. There would be three visual themes – a train, a trial and a field-with-spaceship – that were to be distributed through the four acts. The field theme would also appear as a field-with-dancers. How this was done is best described as mathematical permutation and combination. (Mathematical principle, although not initially intended to recall Einstein, proved to be in keeping with the Einstein motif.) So, Act 1 has the first train and the trial themes (Train 1 and Trial 1). Act 2 has the first field theme and a new train theme (Field 1 and Train 2). Act 3 has a new trial theme and a new field theme (Trial 2 and Field 2). Act 4 pulls the three themes together (Train, Trial and Field, and 'field', this time, is the interior of a spaceship). Wilson named these themes by letters: A for 'train', B for 'trial' and C for 'field', and usually referred to them in this way, naming Act 1 'A1 and B1', and so on for the different combinations. These visual themes mark out the scenes. Thus the first three acts have two scenes each, while the fourth has three, giving a total of nine scenes.

The permutational form of these themes resembles the much more complex musical pattern written according to Glass's techniques of '*additive process* and *cyclical structure*' (Glass, 1988: 58). It is precisely his procedure of repeating say five notes several times, then six, then seven, then eight and so on, that gives the sensation of addition and return in the one stretch of sound. And rhythm is crucial:

> A simple figure can expand and then contract in many different ways, maintaining the same general melodic configuration, but because of the addition (or subtraction) of one note, it takes on a very different rhythmic shape.

(Ibid.)

Glass demonstrates with bars of music from his score how he achieves his various effects (ibid.: 57–62), all of which reveals that his music has a far more compact structure than is implied by its barrage of sound.

It is useful to think, here, of Bach's fugues. After all, Glass is steeped in Bach and in the Western music tradition as a whole. Second, we should think of the sound of the Indian raga system. Glass was deeply influenced by the raga when he worked with Ravi Shankar and his tabla player Alla Rakha. (Shankar is the great Indian sitar player who, in the 1960s, popularised Indian classical music in the West.) The combination of two different music systems, Western and Eastern, accounts for the sounds Glass produces, as in all his compositions. The music for *Einstein* is for two electric organs, three flute players doubling on saxophone and bass clarinet and one solo soprano voice. A chamber chorus of 16 mixed voices carries the vocal music. A solo violinist, whose bushy hair, eyebrows and moustache make him look like Einstein, has featured parts which he plays on the edge of the stage between the instrumentalists and the performers. He is occasionally a useful focus, visual and aural, during a scene change. Sometimes the choir sings from the stage.

The monologues of the libretto were written mostly by Christopher Knowles. Johnson wrote the Old Judge's words for the first trial scene (Act 1) and the love text of Knee Play 5, which concludes the opera. Childs wrote the 'supermarket' monologue that she speaks in the second trial scene (Act 3). The chorus does not have a traditional libretto made up of words. Instead, it sings numbers and the solfège scale ('do, re, mi' and so forth, as distinct from the 'C, D, E' and so forth, of the scale commonly used in Anglo-American societies). Glass had been rehearsing the chorus with numbers and solfège syllables to guide them through the difficulties of remembering the frequently rapidly changing notes and rhythms of his score, in the raga style. As the premiere approached and he had not yet written a single word for the libretto, he decided it was just as well to keep the numbers and notes the singers now knew so well. The way he 'taught the singers became the text. It's also a description of the music' (Glass in Shyer, 1989: 227). Comparing this process to the paintings of Jasper Johns, where the painting does not depict anything, but is the thing itself, Glass acknowledges that his idea 'had roots in the practice of contemporary art' (ibid.). All the vocalists and speakers perform through wire-free microphones hidden on their body.

Movement, apart from the dance sections, is minute. Wilson was to claim, when *Einstein* transferred to the Metropolitan, that the 'smaller the movements were, the more they resounded in that immense theatre' (Lesschaeve, 1977: 219); and he could have said this for most of the large theatres in which *Einstein* was performed afterwards. What is particularly significant about his observation, however, is its negative reference to conventional opera as epitomised for him by Joan Sutherland in *Aida* : 'She is programmed to play "big" in a "big" auditorium – a "big" woman playing on a "big" stage for a "big" public in a "big" opera' (ibid.: 218–19). *Einstein*, by playing on small movement, which Wilson equates with lightness and lack of strain, is his antidote for the visible effort and exaggeration of opera.

Let us recall, in this framework of thought, his distaste for visceral, 'hot' theatre like the Living Theatre. He criticised the latter, at the time of *Einstein*, for its needless stress on the 'actor's effort' (ibid.: 219), and linked this type of overtly physical acting (it could also be described as 'big') to Grotowski of whose influence on the American theatre scene from the mid-1960s he was perfectly aware. Small movement, in his view, not only restrained actors, but also allowed dispassionate presentation of emotion. *Einstein*, then, was Wilson's model for how to do theatre, and that very model served him implicitly later, when he began to stage conventional operas, stripped of their large gestures and emotions, in the 'big' houses of Europe. Among them, eventually, was *Aida* (without Joan Sutherland!) premiered in Brussels in 2002 and subsequently performed at London's Covent Garden in 2003.

BREAKDOWN OF THE WORK

A general overview would be inadequate. Only a detailed breakdown of *Einstein* can allow us to appreciate fully how the constituent elements of its architecture (that is to say, its sustaining structure and outward form) and its content (its thought and inner workings) are put together. All this, together, is nothing other than the 'aesthetics' of the work, which Glass claimed had been his and Wilson's sole concern. Indeed, irrespective of the publicity surrounding it and its cult-like status, which continued to rise over the decades, *Einstein* owes its impact above all else to its artistry. *Einstein* was able to distinguish itself in the experimental 1970s and stand out from among numerous innovative works, and it could still serve as a model of artistic daring 16 years after its first showing, as Glass observes, because it really was a 'performance masterwork' (Howell's evaluation earlier). The fact that audiences continued to be receptive to it suggests that there was enough imagination, inventiveness, craft and skill in *Einstein* to hold their interest, and this despite the changes in value, perception, awareness and taste that necessarily occur as social circumstances change with time and new performance works emerge from them.

KNEE PLAY 1

The first Knee Play lasts 30 minutes and is in progress when the audience enters the auditorium. Two women, one black (Sutton) and the other white (Childs) sit upright behind minimalist 'designer' tables at stage left. They are in a painterly composition in which a square of light projected onto the scrim behind them is echoed by a square of light in front of them extending to the edge of the stage. This scrim will drop for every Knee Play. The women, barely audible, count random numbers. Their fingers slowly perform movements, which could be those of typists or switchboard operators, over their table tops. Three notes are played on two keyboards (electric organs). Each is held for a long time, and soft. One by one, the chorus singers come in and stand in hieratic poses, some facing the audience, some in profile. This occurs 15 minutes into the scene.

When the entire chorus is in the shallow orchestra pit, the lights slowly dim. Spotlights come up on the chorus as they begin to count. One keyboard holds what sounds like one note, but which, in fact, shifts up and down by a semi-tone. The other one repeatedly plays 'do, re, mi'. Childs, in a flat, still barely audible voice, recites something from which she occasionally emphasises a word or a phrase – thus, 'the bus driver', 'red ball' and 'these are the days my friends'. At some point a picture of a child in an old-fashioned suit is projected onto the white square of light. The Knee Play ends abruptly with a blackout.

My close inspection draws attention to some principles that recur throughout the opera:

- the trance-like behaviour of the performers;
- the indeterminacy of action ('typing'?);
- the disconnection between the compositional elements – in this case between action ('typing'?), recitation, picture, music, singing;
- the insignificance of semantics and the emphasis on the sound or quality of words rather than on their actual or potential meaning; and
- the deeply subliminal, invisible effect of everything visible to the eye and ear.

ACT 1, SCENE 1, TRAIN 1

Very fast organ and flute sounds follow the briefest of pauses announced by the blackout. There is a grey backdrop. A small boy stands on a platform protruding from the top of a crane designed in an abstract way. During this scene he occasionally walks along this platform, and throws paper aeroplanes down to the stage.

Childs paces forwards and backwards along a diagonal line – a movement she repeats about 50 times, usually shortening the diagonal towards the end of a sequence before she starts all over again. There is a spring to her step, and she holds a pipe in one hand. Her opposite arm lashes out occasionally to introduce a little variation to her movement more or less along the lines of Glass's additive sound. While she dances, a man scribbles in the air with sharp gestures and sudden stops. He, too, repeats a small range of movements. His back is to the audience, whereas Childs always faces it.

During the course of the scene, Sutton enters from stage left and, with her back to the audience, walks extremely slowly in a straight line to the back of the stage. She then takes a sharp turn, drawing an invisible rectangle as she continues walking. Her walk is deliberate, with knees held high and feet flexed before she places her feet firmly on the floor. This characterises her walking throughout the production. Now and then she breaks her walk with a jerky jump. Later in the scene, three more figures walk unhurriedly, each out of kilter with the other. Sutton suddenly opens a newspaper and walks while reading it. At some point after the second of two sudden blackouts, her arm gesticulates sharply, as if she, like the man, was also writing in the air.

Everyone wears white, short-sleeved shirts (except the man writing, who is in a red shirt), grey baggy pants and black braces and sneakers. Their uniform clearly refers to Einstein, who was continually pictured wearing these clothes. The chorus wears the same uniform throughout the performance. The tones of these no-nonsense costumes blend in with the colours of the sets – reputedly consisting of nothing less than 99 different shades of grey and beige (Quadri, Bertoni and Stearns, 1997: 27).

Fairly early in this scene, a huge cardboard cut-out steam train with a fabulous chimney appears at the back from stage left. It inches its way forward slowly, as if it were peeping out to look. A vertical stream of luminous silver-white light comes down the cyclorama behind the train (Figure 3.1). It is soft-edged, as are drawings of auras, and it cuts the space in half. It is reflected in the floor, which elongates the line of light. Blackout. Lights up. The locomotive has vanished and so has the apparition made of light. But the effect is awesome, like magic. This is probably where the spell of *Einstein* really begins.

The locomotive re-appears two more times in the scene, blowing steam from its chimney. Meanwhile, Childs paces along her line, sometimes slapping her thigh; Sutton does her walk; the man writes; the boy moves about up top; now and then a paper plane glides to the floor; another dancer is immobile at the left stage corner with her leg up, and so on. They are all, performers and objects, 'different energies', as Wilson says, and Childs's particular mini-scene is 'like an electric generator' in respect of everything else (Wilson in Huppert, 1994: 66).

A scrim drops with a picture of a train travelling in a diagonal across a snowy landscape. Someone intones what sound like radio advertisements. None of it is distinct except for the words 'Crazy Eddie', which you could link to the writing figure who does, indeed, appear demented as he stabs the air and, now and then, freezes an upwards-pointing gesture. Childs calls out '1966', someone else, 'What is it?' And the music pounds on, no one in time to it, although Childs's vigorous pace, bounce and drive are the closest to its rhythms and intensity. The cardboard train crawls further along its appointed line each time it appears. On its third appearance, it goes past the silvery stream of light that had returned to the middle of the cyclorama; and it goes almost as far as the crane, changing the configuration of space quite significantly by

Figure 3.1 *Einstein on the Beach* (1976). Photograph by Babette Mangolte, courtesy of Babette Mangolte

its different position. There is another dimension to the train image in so far as it refers to Einstein's well-known love of trains. However, spectators who are not aware of this bit of biographical information lose nothing of the scene's strange enchantment. Allusions in a Wilson work do not have to be recognised because his work is never geared primarily towards semantic meaning.

The music stops abruptly. The train edges back and disappears into the wings. The human figures seem to vanish into thin air. The crane breaks apart: its platform goes up into the flies, its body into the wings. 'Crazy Eddie' looks sideways, holds still and resumes writing. The nocturnal charcoals, greys and blues that appeared on the cyclorama every time the train appeared and looked more and more like a brewing storm, now become much darker, their emotional tone changing from mystery to menace. The luminous stream of light just stays there, growing brighter as the rest deepens. The same happens to its reflection on the floorboards.

People start walking about, marking the floor. They bring in what, in the semi-obscurity, look like geometric shapes. Some of them are fitted together like books ends, and circles are placed on top of them. Others, now rectangular, are laid down flat on the stage and covered with a long white sheet. All this activity is unhurried. The organ hums, as if stuck on a note. Spectators begin to suspect – rightly – that this is a scene change. A spotlight is on 'Crazy Eddie' who keeps writing or points his finger diagonally towards the wings until a rectangular black box is lowered from the flies, cutting the magic stream of light like a 't'. The magic light snaps out. Then there is a minute of blackout. The scene change lasts 10 minutes in all, during which time you have been mesmerised by the light.

The whole of the first scene beautifully encapsulates Wilson's life-long concerns:

- his focus on space, time and timing;
- his design along a plethora of lines – vertical (the crane, Sutton, the light), horizontal (the train, the crane platform, bent arms and legs) and diagonal (Childs, who shifts the diagonal further and further away from the centre);
- his composition by layers – the images are one layer, the music/soundscore is another, the language another, the dances another, and so on;

- his disinterest in characters, replacing them with performers doing physical actions;
- his fascination with simultaneous, unrelated actions;
- his predilection for non-communication between figures so much so that they all appear distant, isolated and unrelated to anyone else;
- his complete commitment to the autonomy of light, how it is shaped into planes (in later works, it will be planes of vivid colour), and how it illuminates parts of the body – here the hand of the immobile figure at stage right, or the pointing hand of 'Crazy Eddie';
- his principles of juxtaposition and counterpoint; and
- his principles of allusion, ellipsis and association.

ACT 1, SCENE 2, TRIAL 1

The scene, emptied of people, opens by drawing your gaze towards what was the rectangular black box and is now a horizontal beam of fluorescent light suspended above the stage. At first the whole space is in charcoals and black. It is soon washed in Wilson's inimitable blue. An iridescent light covers a low flat bed below two assembled 'book ends', which are, in fact, a desk lit at each end by two round lamps. The fluorescent beam, the desk, the two white screens behind it and the bed are all the same length, their geometric symmetry creating a feeling of calmness. Another iridescent light illuminates a high, metal chair standing near one of these lamps. Two groups of people enter in Einstein uniform. The group on the left stands in profile in two rows. The four on the right sit on two metal benches, their backs to the audience. This opening occurs to the quiet tones of the two organs and the women in the choir singing what sounds like '3, 4'.

Everything in this 45-minute scene is slow, including the descent of panels, circles and scrims that layer the whole and recall the constructivist design of celebrated German expressionist films, most notably Fritz Lang's 1927 *Metropolis*. Childs and her 'double' do some stretchbend dance movements before they sit at stage right, one behind the other, at school desks. A man at stage right, whose briefcase is outlined by fluorescent tubes, is stuck on the spot. He looks funnier still later on, when he swings his briefcase, or when someone briskly walks in, briskly straightens his tie and briskly leaves. Eventually two judges come in and sit at the desk. They are the young white Knowles and the elderly black Johnson.

We know from the previous chapters that slowness in Wilson's productions is never stillness. In this scene, small but pronounced hand movements first move with the slow action and then counterpoint it. Childs and her double gesticulate with their fingers: perhaps they 'spool', 'weave', 'file their nails' and also 'type', as in the 'typing' of Knee Play 1. Are they stenographers? The chorus – for it is they who stand at stage right – also look as if they are 'typing' while they drone out their syllables, sopranos followed by the men's voices. The difficulty for the singers lies in how their gestures do not follow the tempi of their singing, which means that their movements constantly work against their voices. Someone is reading a book. The figures at stage left stay seated and dance only with their arms and torsos throughout the scene. The Old Judge, who is very still, moves only when he beats the desk with his gavel: three times each on six, well spaced occasions, each beat given its full measure. These sounds highlight the fact that Wilson calculates precisely the tempo of the scene as a whole.

While the scene is consistently in slow motion, regardless of the 'typing' gestures that continue, uninterrupted, its music changes pace, going from a drone at the beginning to a repeated sawing up and down a scale by the 'Einstein' violinist, who is seated in a spotlight at the front-right side of the stage. He plays two amplified solo sequences (one lasting 20 minutes). Each ends abruptly, the second in mid-flight. The choir, some of whom sing from the stage, speeds up, as if 'echoing' the violin, led by the fast and strong beat of the instrumental ensemble.

The blasts of sound counter coolly spoken words. Sutton may here be a lawyer figure, and can be heard intermittently saying 'Mr Bojangles' and 'So if you see any of those baggy pants'. On other occasions she yells 'Go' (or is it 'No'?) or repeats 'gun, gun, gun', usually in different rhythms broken up by pauses of various length. Childs dressed as Einstein is on a high metal chair. Johnson and Knowles alternately repeat six times with authority, 'This court of common pleas is now in session.' Each pronouncement is preceded by the beat of Johnson's hammer. All of it speaks to the senses rather than to our rational minds. Towards the end of the scene, Johnson delivers – deadpan – a humorous parody of small-town feminism. (In France his speech, the only one in the production in French, seemed to send up the cliché of French lovers.) 'Crazy Eddie' has somehow re-appeared, still writing into space at stage left.

Meanwhile, a number of shapes have come down from the flies: two tall panels, which both frame and throw into relief the judges' desk;

two more with indistinct pictures on them; the face of a white clock without hands – a timeless clock which stops its descent in the middle of the constructivist, geometrically organised space behind the judges' desk; another clock higher up; a gigantic test tube; a portrait that could be young Einstein; a transparent scrim on which is projected a classical nude. A large black disc glides in from the side and slowly eclipses the white clock (probably an allusion to the eclipse that corroborated Einstein's theory) (Figure 3.2). The scrim with nude drops towards the end of the scene; the white bed is translucent behind it. When it drops, the stage is swathed in grey-blue. Lights out. The organ and 'Einstein' continue to play in the dark.

KNEE PLAY 2

The violinist fiddles away right through the interlude. A bright square like the one in the first Knee Play illuminates Childs and Sutton who are on their chairs, talking quite fast, out of sync. Their various movements, by contrast, are very measured and include bending forwards and crouching on the floor before they return to their positions on the chairs. The text concerns a sailboat, a balloon and 'a Phonic Centre' that has 'contactless lenses and the new soft lenses' to 'answer your problem'. This interlude ends with a spectacular movement requiring perfect muscular co-ordination and control. Both women lean sideways and balance on one buttock on their chairs with the other one lifted, while their knees are up and their arms bent upwards. They call out '1905'. A photograph of Einstein was projected, at some point, onto the square behind them. The date seems as random as anything else, so it matters little whether you know or not that 1905 is the publication date of Einstein's article 'On the Electrodynamics of Moving Bodies' which is the basis of his theory of relativity and which changed forever our sense of the universe.

ACT 2, SCENE 1, FIELD 1

The first of the opera's two dance sequences – both in a contemporary dance idiom – is an exciting display of velocity, agility, lightness and precision in an empty stage. Eight dancers enter and exit in ones and twos or form configurations of three, five and eight. They leap, turn,

Figure 3.2 *Einstein on the Beach* (1976). Photograph by Babette Mangolte, courtesy of Babette Mangolte

circle, skip, spin and jump across the entire space with their arms usually out in a relaxed second position. It is a joyous, buoyant dance whose sense of freedom is exhilarating. Blackout.

ACT 2, SCENE 2, TRAIN 2

Warm low lights go up on the back of a railway carriage in the middle of the stage. A quarter moon hangs in the night sky. By the end of the scene it will be full, before an eclipse blots it out. A man and a woman are in profile. He walks out onto the end of the carriage, which could be from a Western movie. She follows him and they lip-sync a duet sung by a soprano and a tenor in the pit. The duet, 'happy lucky lover', is sung very quickly in repeated combinations ('happy lucky', 'lucky lover', 'happy lucky lover') which alternate with '1, 2, 3' also sung very quickly. The lovers are in evening dress, she (Sutton) in an exquisite white gown. The event is too delicately presented to be a parody of something like 'By the light of the silvery moon'. Yet the temptation to see it as parody is almost unavoidable, especially because the duet begins to sound more absurd and quite ironic the longer you listen to it. When the eclipse occurs, it recalls, with some humour, the eclipse of the preceding act. Many in my 1992 audience laughed.

The lovers return to their compartment. The light on the carriage gradually grows smaller, creating the illusion of a train receding into the distance. The elegant lady, smiling, points a gun at her lover. This image demonstrates how Wilson elides a human drama, missing its details so as to sum it up cogently in one shot (no pun intended with the gun!). Blackout. A small light focuses on the carriage – now empty – to indicate its increasing distance. The image feels like a coda to the drama which has taken place without words, 'danced', as it were, in a dream-like state that is transferred to the spectators. So absorbing is the dream atmosphere by the end of the scene that the sound coming from the pit becomes something of an intrusion, a noise penetrating your consciousness to wake you up. Meanwhile, a woman at stage right has interminably held a curiously disjointed arabesque, facing three quarters to the audience. Two spots of light, like eyes glowing in the dark, hang in the sky after the eclipse. Second blackout.

In Train 2, Wilson changes perspective from the front to the back of the train. By now spectators have looked at the stage pictures from numerous different angles of vision. These shifts of perspective and perception suggest that Wilson materialises in the production that spin-off from Einstein's theory of relativity which had hit the general public early in the twentieth century: namely, there is no one way of looking at things because truth, like time, is not fixed; how you perceive is relative to where you are in space and time. This, if anything, is the *philosophical* content of the opera.

KNEE PLAY 3

Another variation on the first Knee Play. Sutton and Childs are back in their bright, white square, this time with their back to the audience (a shift of perspective, once again). To all intents and purposes, the two women manipulate a control board covered with twisted circles of light. The chorus is below them, lit up as it was at the beginning of the production; and the singers return to their 'do, re mi', operating some sort of invisible machine with their hands in the air as they sing.

ACT 3, SCENE 1, TRIAL 2

The scene is as long as the first trial scene. However, it is a deconstruction of its predecessor in that the sets, which are those of Trial 1, are pulled apart in full view. The benches belonging to the four dancers are pulled away by strings – a technique Wilson was to exploit increasingly in his rock operas, grand operas and such fundamentally operatic solo pieces as *Orlando* and *Hamlet*. One half of the bed is pulled closer to the wings by strings. It is then carried off, as are one half of the judge's desk, his chair, the metal high chair standing near the desk and other bits of furniture. Scrims and panels go up into the flies. Later, the school desks at stage right are pulled away by magic, alias strings.

Wilson's delight in dismantling the stage is equal only to the business of reconstructing it. An enormous scrim the width of the stage comes down. A grille half the width of the stage, and whose vertical black bars suggest a prison, drops down at stage left. This and more will deconstruct towards the end of the scene, leaving an open stage for Childs's final monologue, which she speaks on the high chair that was also used for Trial 1.

The process in its entirety is a potent demonstration of modernist theatricality as developed by Meyerhold during his constructivist phase, when he divided up his stage into different planes and levels, and by Oscar Schlemmer in whose performance work at the Bauhaus dancers, actors and objects were interchangeable parts of form in motion. Performance, for Schlemmer, was essentially a matter of moving architecture (Gropius and Wensinger, 1961: 17–35). Wilson's process is concerned with constructing space so that it constantly moves while providing multiple planes for action. The 'prison' grille, for example, creates several planes for action to occur – behind it, to the front and to its sides. The bed is another action plane when Childs uses it. Meanwhile, the grille, the bed and the edge of the desk provide a passageway for movement. At the same time, Wilson constructs space for the purposes of architectural shaping and perspective, pictorial balance, and visual impact.

Wilson's deconstruction of what he constructs with such care is not confined to architecture and objects, but includes movement, as well. The scene begins as if it had been suspended in time because the judges are behind their bench, as in Trial 1. They duly leave, separately, the second judge when the set breaks up conclusively. The four dancers, who had come in with a march-like step to resume their position on their benches, stay just long enough to remind spectators that they had been there before. Then they leave, deconstructing the movements they had made earlier with their upper body and arms. No one speaks during this piece of breaking and remaking.

Trial 2, although slow in its first half, is busy (and much busier than my synopsis, although it summarises the essential). The chorus repeat their earlier 'typing' or telephone-operator gestures, as do two women at the school desks. Childs comes in, demur in a white dress, and gets into the bed. When she comes out, she puts on a black jacket and black pants, and pulls out a machine gun, which she first points towards the chorus and then towards the audience. In the meantime, Sutton does a series of her trance-walks in various directions.

Unless you were informed, you would be hard pressed to say that the woman in black was a reference to Patty Hearst, the young newspaper heiress who was kidnapped in 1974 by a guerrilla-style terrorist group and brainwashed by her captors to turn against wealth and privilege. She did so with a vengeance by participating in an armed bank robbery and appearing as a poster girl with a machine gun, ready for battle. The Hearst case was infamous, and Childs, in the 1976 original of the scene, had been described as striking 'poses like those of Patty Hearst, familiar from recent magazine covers' (Flakes, 1976: 79). These are topical references, and could only seem obscure at a later date. While Childs behaves oddly (or alludes to Hearst, if you know it), the 'Einstein' violinist sits in his place at the edge of the stage, spotlighted as before.

As usual, the texts are aleatory. Childs repeatedly recites (some 35 times, starting from the bed) in a cool, clear voice the litany she had written herself on how she was in 'this prematurely airconditioned supermarket' full of bathing caps (colours enumerated), 'but I was reminded of the fact that I had been avoiding the beach' – the only reference to the production's title in the whole production. Unlike preceding and following recitations, this one is distinct, its every word and intonation building a line of sound, none of it obliterated by the music. Wilson's idea that repetition liberates performers from anxiety – they can simply *do* without having to think about it – is here demonstrated by Childs's vocal and physical ease. After the machine gun sequence, Sutton-as-lawyer speaks of 'Mr Bojangles' again, as she had done in Trial 1. Childs-as-witness is on the high chair in her white dress. She recites her second text ('I feel the earth move' by Knowles), which ends with a list of names and times. She repeats this long soliloquy ritualistically three times. Its effect is hypnotic. She ends the scene alone on the stage.

Who is on trial? Is it Patty Hearst? (She *was* tried.) Einstein, for opening the door to the atom bomb? No one in particular? Stefan Brecht, when studying the 1976 version, indicates that Einstein was a dreamer and thus the bed can be associated with him. But, to his mind, the bed, not Einstein, is on trial (Brecht, 1994: 347), and his guess is as surreal as any other. For Brecht, Childs's crawling into the bed 'was in the petty contemporary vein of arbitrary action' (ibid.: 346) and a 'remnant of some fleeting plot-idea' (ibid.: 348) that Wilson had had (presumably at some stage in the work's development).

When all is said and done, Trial 2 veers towards camp or kitsch – the beginnings of a recurrent feature of Wilson's music theatre, grand opera included. Wilson does not always manage it with aplomb. Thus camp/kitsch could be said to be merely decorative in *Einstein on the Beach*, whereas it is structurally intrinsic to *The Black Rider* and *Woyzeck*. It is so thoroughly over-the-top in *The Black Rider* that it is persuasive, and is powerful by its incongruity in *Woyzeck*. His opera productions carry it to varying degrees with varying results. *Aida*, for instance, might well be without Joan Sutherland, but it brims over with 'big' camp/kitsch, especially in dance sequences, which makes a mockery of this opera itself.

The music of Trial 2, on the other hand, is sensational. It roars and yowls, cascades and thunders, and rolls and darts and dives, changing its dynamics when you least expect it, and unexpectedly cutting out. You are surprised, although you should not be, given that Glass cuts off the music as dramatically as Wilson cuts his lights. There is a neat transition in the music to clarinet and saxophone when Childs, in an opera-style recitative, talks over these instruments without effort, and closes the scene.

ACT 3, SCENE 2, FIELD 2

Blackout to start. Lights up on all eight dancers with their backs to the audience. The cyclorama at the back is a sky. They face us one by one, brilliantly executing balletic *ronds de jambe*. In fact, many of their steps are from ballet – *jetés*, *grands battements*, *fouetés*, *pirouettes* – as happens in various kinds of contemporary dance, the difference from the former lying in the looseness of the dancers' bodies. The dancers mostly dance together to give a sense of mass, but their dance is fast, relentless, like 'Einstein' who saws away in his usual spot (Figure 3.3). Could the chorus really be reiterating 'lovey dovey' at top speed? Glass and Wilson play enough pranks in the work (like 'lucky lover' in Train 2) for this to be possible. Five minutes before the end of the dance the light turns blue and a gauze scrim descends, covered with stars. It looks beautiful, and could be another joke: 'lovey dovey', indeed! The dancers continue dancing, visible, but veiled and distanced by the scrim in another play of perspective.

KNEE PLAY 4

Blackout. Silence. 'Einstein' – spotlighted – starts to fiddle away. The preceding scene and this Knee Play merge as one. Six of the chorus are lit up standing in the pit and singing 'do, re, mi, fa, sol'. (They have gone further up the scale, which is surely meant to be funny. Later they go backwards, down the scale.) Childs and Sutton are back in their square, only this time they gyrate and swivel slowly on high plexiglass tables, their legs 'swimming' in the air. At some point, they are lit from above and below in such a way as to make the glass disappear and to suggest that they are weightless, floating in space. Their stomach muscles are their centre of gravity, for this dance requires enormous physical control.

Figure 3.3 *Einstein on the Beach* (1976). Photograph by Babette Mangolte, courtesy of Babette Mangolte

How the action looks to the spectator and how it feels for the performer are quite different. As David Warrilow from Mabou Mines remarked of his performance in Wilson's *The Golden Windows* at BAM in 1985:

> You're on a rake and you have to walk, calmly, slowly, steadily upstage: it may look cool and beautiful, but it's a saga of muscular and balance diffi- culty.... There is in Bob's work almost an expectation of perfection. That creates a lot of stress and that's the last thing the audience should see.
>
> (cited in Shyer, 1989: 21)

Anything but stress is conveyed either by the dancers or the singers, who run their syllables perfectly. The Knee Play ends with a gag when the singers pretend to brush their teeth and then, unexpectedly, stick their tongue out (Figure 3.4). You may not realise until after the show

Figure 3.4 *Einstein on the Beach* (1976). Photograph by T. Charles Erickson [1992], courtesy of T. Charles Erickson

that this action imitates a famous photograph of Einstein sticking out his tongue at the photographers. But it is not important if you miss the association between the image in the performance and the image that inspired it. The moment is indeterminate, leaving you free to choose your own associations, as Wilson intended. The connection between an image of tongues stuck out and Einstein is significant only when you do a formal analysis of the piece, which is what we are engaged in here.

ACT 4, SCENE 1, TRAIN 3 (WITH BUILDING)

The scene lasts 10 minutes. The organ scurries in the dark before an enormous building painted on a backdrop, which is a cross between a Renaissance palace and an Industrial Age power station, appears at centre stage. A man in one of its upper windows writes, unperturbed, at a board. A child rides in on his skate board, followed by one, two and finally a total of 24 people dressed in Einstein uniform who gaze ahead, each in a different direction until they all look up at the scribbling figure. They walk off, one by one. Brecht claims that Wilson makes the scene 'a representation of reality' and argues that it is 'an actual gathering of unrelated undistinguished people out for a stroll happening onto this great man [Einstein] at work' (Brecht, 1994: 354). The man goes out.

ACT 4, SCENE 2, TRIAL 3 (THE BED)

The lights go down and the drop goes up in the dark. The organ cuts off suddenly and picks up a Bach-style fugue almost immediately. A luminous band placed horizontally where the foot of the bed was in Trial 2 shines in the darkness. Here begins a 20-minute choreography for this column of light that might as well be a piece of sculpture, but performs like an actor. (And there are no other performers on stage during its 'flight'.) The column slowly levitates, tilts to one side, hovers and goes through a 45-degree angle until it reaches a vertical position (Figure 3.5). It then hangs in space just above the floor and starts rising vertically. Once it has reached mid-height, it progressively grows shorter, creating the illusion that it is receding into the distance, further and further away until it fades out. The effect is hallucinatory, and the audience totally spellbound. We are meant to be reminded of the magic stream of light in Train 1, the cross-reference between the two, as between the fragments of a dream, being part of the surrealist 'method' that was to become a Wilson trademark.

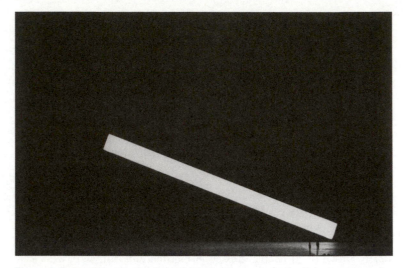

Figure 3.5 *Einstein on the Beach* (1976). Photograph by Babette Mangolte, courtesy of Babette Mangolte

The whole of this amazing ascension is accompanied by the organ, which holds a single note very softly. The organ eventually stops, starts again and changes pitch and rhythm. An aria for soprano begins about 10 minutes into the light's performance. The soprano sustains her two or three notes without words softly, gently, much like the organ. It is small wonder that the American newspaper critics cited at the beginning of this chapter spoke of *Einstein* as 'religious' and mystical' and that Rockwell, who was deeply moved by the production, took light, with its merger of symbolic connotations and scientific meanings as energy and power, to be the core subject of the work.

ACT 4, SCENE 3, FIELD 3 (INTERIOR OF SPACESHIP)

Act 4 is different from the preceding acts in that its scenes are not crisply demarcated, but flow into each other. The flow into this scene is an upsurge. The organ begins to 'wa-wa' and fluorescent light jumps nervously along tubes placed in parallel diagonals on what appears to be a wall. A man (Wilson) paces back and forth as did Childs in Train 1 and appears to be guiding something or someone in with two torches, the way a plane is guided in from a runway. Someone else is doing semaphoric gestures. A glass elevator with a young boy and a clock inside it emerges from the floor, steam billowing out from its tail, and goes upwards. 'Einstein' sits silently in a spotlight in his usual place.

The minute 'Einstein' starts on his electric violin – his and everybody else's sound amplified to the full – the whole thing takes off. Wilson's torch dance becomes faster and faster; the semaphore-person moves frantically; the elevator goes up and down; a capsule near the top of whatever we are looking at glides backwards and forwards along a hor-izontal line; flashing lights show that the whole contraption, virtually the length and height of the stage, is a burnt-gold colour, three stories high and divided into 15 cubicles; bodies gesticulate in shadows; a scrim falls and a small rocket-spaceship is rapidly pulled along it, on a string, diagonally upwards; voices; numbers; roaring music; beat of music; urgency. You realise that what you are looking at resembles the control board of a spacecraft that you have seen in science fiction films or comics. And your impression is confirmed when the lights go mad. Circle-swirls and vertical broken lines flash on and off like so many unstoppable, unreadable symbols spat out by a computer.

Two plastic bubbles on the floor spew out smoke. Childs and Sutton, who are cool and collected, crawl out towards the audience and bend into the floor. As they crawl, a gauze drop falls behind them. Wilson keeps dancing. You begin to make out the shape of the earth from the grey and white design on the gauze, and realise with a jolt that the image is of an atomic explosion. A grey plane flies at the top left of the drop. At the bottom left is a small dinosaur. The music snaps off. Are we at the beginning (dinosaur) and at the end of time (atomic explosion)? We could well be, for the whole spectacular finale has an apocalyptic air. It is certainly contrived, certainly artificial, but its energy is irresistible.

KNEE PLAY 5

The music resumes immediately with single, spaced-out notes. Its volume has dropped considerably. The gauze curtain showing the explosion lingers a while and then goes up. Another one comes down. The women slowly lift the upper part of their bodies, get up and walk backwards to the seats brought in for them at stage right. They sit apart peacefully, their fingers 'typing' slowly, as in the opening Knee Play. The music is light. The violin comes in, sweetly and gently. A bus similar to the locomotive of Train 1 enters at stage left. Its driver (Johnson) is warmly lit up from below. He speaks of two lovers on a park bench and ends his tale with a mild joke on kissing.

SUMMING UP

It is only when *Einstein* is analysed closely that its performance principles become apparent. The actual experience of the work is nowhere near as clear, not least because the action on stage looks arbitrary. We usually cannot decipher on the spot the numerous sensations we feel during a performance. This natural difficulty is compounded by *Einstein* primarily because the influx of sensations prompted by it either causes confusion, or is so great – even overwhelming, as transpires from the awestruck tone of critical reviews – that it cannot be assessed immediately. Only after the event can an appropriate overview be taken of the production's system of presentation by layers or separate planes, which is reminiscent of how Wilson's beloved Cézanne applies paint to canvas. Wilson explains that in making *Einstein* he 'thought a lot about gestures and movements as something separate, of the lights as separate', of the decor, drops and furniture as separate and so on (Obenhaus, 1985); and the result is a juxtaposition of what is separate – most striking, perhaps, in the juxtaposition between the spoken texts and the situations in which they are spoken.

This separation procedure also involves looking from multiple angles of vision along the multiple planes (or separate elements) held in one frame, which is a cubist technique invented by Cézanne. By the same token, it allows Wilson to use the modes he borrows from painting – portrait, still life and landscape – in a particularly pronounced way. Thus, in *Einstein*, they provide him with *structurally* inscribed perspectives: the knee plays are the close-up portraits; the train and trial scenes provide the middle-range perspective of still life; the dance sections and the spaceship's interior provide the long view of landscapes.

Einstein is additionally difficult to process during performance because its themes are not mediated by such standard elements of drama as character, dialogue and plot. The production's themes are articulated through images, colour, gesture, rhythm, movement, sound, objects and garments. And they rely, sometimes quite heavily, on the collage techniques of echo, variation, inversion and abstraction – all evident in the collages made in New York from the 1950s to the early 1970s. Wilson, however, leaves the rough-and-tumble of the loft culture that had spawned them to produce, in *Einstein*, a formal, polished piece whose home is European modernist art (as my earlier references to the Bauhuas, and so on, have suggested).

Collage, in *Einstein*, relies on neat organisation. The train theme is repeated in the building which, looked at intently, proves to be an 'enlarged' variation, in a phantasmagoric rather than realistic vein, of the image of the back of the train in Train 2. Arguably, the whole range of images of means of transport – walking, train, plane, bus, spaceship – is a collage of the production's motifs of time and space, and of the movement in them; and, arguably, these images dot out, in the dislocated fashion of collage, the transition from the steam age to the age of space travel (which is the time span of Einstein's life. Wilson might well have been mentally inserting *Einstein* into his earlier *Life and Times of* . . . series of productions).

The spaceship theme operates in a similar fashion. The toy rocket, which is seen from the outside, is an inversion in miniature of the spaceship seen earlier from the inside. Childs and Sutton crawl out of bubbles and could be cosmonauts emerging from their capsules. The plexiglass elevator could be inside a spaceship flying through the cosmos (but could also be inside an apartment block). The dance as a spaceship (Field 2) is far more cryptic. Only when the whole context is reconstructed is it possible to see that the velocity, lightness and travel of the dance could be an abstract 'representation' of the trajectory of a spaceship.

These examples throw up a third group of points, which concerns the absence of linear narrative in *Einstein*. Narrative connections can be drawn between the lights-gone-mad of the spaceship and the spat out 'cosmonauts'. The latter can be seen as 'survivors' of a cosmic accident or, equally, of the atomic blast pictured on the scrim. The images of Trial 2 are elliptical, but nevertheless suggest some kind of story. (I have spoken, for example, of Sutton as a 'lawyer figure'.) Scholars have noted allegedly explicit references to Patty Hearst in Trial 2, and have given them a narrative form (Brecht, 1994: 348–51; Holmberg, 1996: 11). Yet, there is no pressing need to construct a narrative from any of these bits and their potential 'stories' about cosmonauts, atom bombs or terrorists. Whatever Wilson's private allusions may have been in the making of his opera, they operate as allusions *in* the work, which is a piece of experimental theatre far closer to the happenings and performance art of Wilson's formative years than to canonical theatre with its narrative sequences, consequences and resolutions. Too literal a dependency on the production's allusions deprives it of its rich ambiguity.

And this leads to a fourth group of observations regarding the particular character of *Einstein*. The production fully demonstrates Wilson's distinction between the 'interior screen' (or 'interior reflection', as discussed in Chapter 2) and the 'exterior screen'. The 'exterior screen' is the production's semiotic system, including its numerous allusions to Einstein. There are more allusions to add to those already mentioned. Einstein was a good amateur violinist (!), smoked a pipe (Childs in Train 1) and declared after the first atom bomb was dropped that he 'wouldn't be a scientist but a plumber or a peddler' (cited in Holmberg, 1996: 11) if he had his life all over again. The high chair of Trial 1 and Trial 2 is made of plumbing pipes, which Glass claims is Wilson's allusion to Einstein's declaration (ibid.; Glass, 1988: 34). If this is the case, the chair speaks visually rather than verbally about what Einstein said in words. It is a pictorial transposition of language.

The 'interior screen' is each individual's way of processing within his/her sphere of understanding, which is also deeply subliminal. Wilson's own 'interior screen' – what has personal resonance for him – has to do with Einstein's life and achievements, but spectators may not catch any of it at all. Spectators may not have the slightest idea about Einstein, which was likely the case of the young people watching the show in 1992, who had not grown up with the Einstein myth, as Wilson and Glass had done in the 1950s. Furthermore, spectators engage with the 'exterior screen' of any work. When it has as much on display to captivate the senses as *Einstein*, it can override the 'interior screen' and compel attention to itself as 'pure form', as form that spectators do not need to fill with personal meanings to take pleasure from it.

The production's capacity to generate such great interest in its surface that the resonances beneath the surface become more or less incidental may well be what Wilson meant by his critical remark in 1984. *Einstein*, he said, was 'from another period – very static, and flat . . . very two-dimensional' (cited at the beginning of this chapter; 'flat' and 'two-dimensional' imply 'surface'). As the production unfolds, its monumental scale, technical feats, stunning juxtapositions and sheer hypnotic beauty are compelling of their own accord (even when considered 'two-dimensional'). So prolific and powerful are these features of the 'exterior screen' that they can efface your 'interior screen', sending you on a 'high', or into a trance, or to sleep – if, of course, they do not send you out of the theatre bored out of your brain.

Paradoxically, Wilson's play of associations, allusions and ellipses on the 'exterior screen' – for they *do* appear here – raises the question as to whether their dynamic can be anything other than that of 'pure form'. This, we know from the preceding chapters, is the trickiest area of Wilson's aesthetics. The 'pure form' of his earliest pieces from *The King of Spain* to *Deafman Glance* provided the 'mental environments' that Brecht believes distinguished these silent works (Brecht, 1994: 360). Association, and so on, were there in free fall, not attached to ideas of content. However, *Einstein* is quite different in that it seeks to connect form to content in some way. In this respect, it is a turning point in Wilson's aesthetics.

We saw that the question of what *Einstein* is about, *the* fundamental point for discussions of content, did not concern newspaper reviewers. It became a cause for critique in scholarly accounts. Brecht maintains that, although *Einstein* is 'not without content', it 'took one in as pure surface, aesthetically'; and its structure is a 'mere formality', which makes its themes 'meaningless' (Brecht, 1994: 360, 375). Michael Vanden Heuvel argues that, in *Einstein*, Wilson 'works to agitate various sets of conflicting attitudes and desires: popular and esoteric art . . . form and content, sensualism and spirituality, rationalism and irrationalism' (Vanden Heuvel, 1993: 176). Here and increasingly in his productions, Wilson wants 'both the powerlessness and the lack of referentiality of pure spectacle, along with the clarity and order of rigid form and significant content' (ibid.). In *Einstein* he fails to 'find a fruitful dynamic' (ibid.: 177) between this tension and all his other 'conflicting attitudes'. Moreover, while attempting to find a form capable of bringing such 'conflicting attitudes' together, Wilson 'gets caught between the almost pure surrealism of his earliest work and the limited conventions of opera and the Broadway musical' (ibid.). The whole of this argument rests on the assumption that *Einstein*'s allegedly 'conflictual attitudes' are a matter of binary oppositions.

However, the contrary can be argued, namely, that Wilson neither thinks in terms of conflictual (or binary) 'sets', nor do conflictual (or binary) 'sets' appear in the work: his goal is the syncretic co-existence of disparate elements, and this can accommodate 'pure' surrealism along with the conventions of opera and musicals. The syncretism of *Einstein*, the first of a series of syncretic productions by Wilson, prompts the description of 'hybrid' and 'crossover' for them. Furthermore, it can be argued that Wilson definitely did succeed in combining 'lack of referentiality' and 'significant content' not through any purported 'sets', but – crucially for my argument – via his loose play of allusions, ellipses and associations. All of these allusions, and so on, work in the same way towards the same ends and perform a dual function, formal *and* contentual, rather than a dichotomous one. I am not referring to the bread-and-butter allusions to pipe and plumbing, but to the more sophisticated ones that refer to the 'significant content' of the dynamics of space, time, light and everything else that we have identified as relevant to Einstein's theory of relativity. For, apart from implying content, these very allusions refer, at the same time, and in a cubist/constructivist way, to the mechanisms of the production. The mechanisms on display are by no means mindless since what they do and how they do it are the embodiment of conceptual thought. Put differently, this means that showing how, say, light is handled demonstrates Wilson's idea of light as he puts the idea into practice. And this mechanism-cum-concept is most definitely also the 'content' of *Einstein*.

Where light is concerned specifically, it is impossible to ignore the structural, conceptual and contentual importance of the production's frequent blackouts. These blackouts create a type of conversation with light, suggesting by their removal of light just how indispensable light is to all living matter and, indeed to the universe as *universe*. (Einstein's understanding of the cosmos can thus also be seen in this particular aspect of the production's construction.) Alongside this grandiose cosmic vision is Wilson's passion for light in the theatre whose ramifications, artistically and technologically, have been discussed in the preceding chapter. It suffices to repeat here that Wilson always uses light to convey emotion openly in a way that he prevents his performers from doing. And he prevents them from doing it because he associates open expression of emotion with exaggeration as well as with the 'actor's effort' in overdrive of the kind that he thinks characterises the performances of the Living Theatre or of the Grotowskian actor (Lesschaeve, 1977: 219).

Emotion, then, is deflected away from the performers who, in any case, do not psychologically represent characters but configure them (a consequence, we know, of Wilson's dislike of 'naturalist' theatre). It is invested, instead, in light which, by its tones and degrees of intensity, tells us of the emotional state not necessarily of the 'characters' – *Einstein* is conspicuous by their absence – but of the stage events as such. One of these events in *Einstein* is the stream of light in Train 1 around which a range of different hues keeps shifting the scene's emotional colouring 'from mystery to menace', as I have put it earlier. We have seen from various examples in the preceding chapter how, after *Einstein*, Wilson displaces the emotions of characters with light, making light an emotionally eloquent and emotionally catalytic force.

Another factor plays its part in the way Wilson deals with 'content' whose meaning for Wilson does not coincide with the meaning attributed to this word by his critics. Content, for Wilson, is what, at the beginning of my analytical breakdown of the production, I have called 'thought and inner workings'. Misunderstandings and disagreements over the meaning of the term 'content' in respect of Wilson's work are real enough. Yet he averts in *Einstein* what can be seen to be a problematical aspect of his aesthetics as a whole precisely because, by the sheer force of circumstances, 'pure form' and 'content' coincide in it. In other words, Wilson's preoccupations in *Einstein* with space, time and light as form *and* content fit in with Einstein's concerns regarding space, time and light. It is a happy 'fit'. This remarkable concordance also makes *Einstein on the Beach* a landmark in performance history.

4

PRACTICAL EXERCISES

It would be unreasonable to assume that the exercises suggested in the pages to follow are a direct reproduction of what Wilson does in workshops and rehearsals. Wilson does not have a training system for actors, directors and stage and light designers, whose various activities he carries out himself with great skill. We have had a glimpse of the incredible range of people with whom he has worked across the globe in different cultural contexts, group affiliations and languages. All have nurtured him in some way, as he has them, in the inspiring and creative interchange that makes the theatre, in all its multiple forms and hybridising processes, a collaborative endeavour virtually like no other. Such an extraordinary, polyphonic experience of the world of the theatre has given Wilson an intimate knowledge of its workings, which this section of my book cannot begin to convey fully.

Wilson works systematically, but does not attempt to put his imagination and techniques into a manual for practitioners. Nor does he try to transmit them in a formal learning structure at the Watermill Centre, which he treats as a laboratory. Professionals and students meet here with ideas that they share and test in open situations, grouping together according to what they think they need to find out at a given moment. Some may wish to focus on aspects of performance. Others may gravitate around a participant's ongoing or proposed architectural or design project. They are free to contribute with questions and proposals from their own field of expertise or with simple observations out of sheer curiosity and no expertise at all. Watermill workshops, which are workshops in the loosest sense of this term, involve people coming from very different horizons at varying points in their development. All, as they mix and mingle their perspectives, provide the resources for the intergeneric exploration – Wilson calls it 'interdisciplinary research' – that he had envisaged for his Centre from its very inception.

My introduction suggests that Wilson, although interested in the learning process, is not a teacher like, say, Michael Chekhov and Jacques Lecoq. This means that we cannot draw on specifically Wilsonian exercises elaborated by him through pedagogical means for artistic ends. Nor can we refer to a school of thought carried on by his students, as is true of the two men cited. What we *can* do, and can do fruitfully, is extrapolate intelligently from his practice and what he says about it. We can invent exercises inspired by his workshops, rehearsals and observations. And we can devise material from the many examples in the preceding chapters of how he went about achieving what he did in his productions. There is plenty there from which to choose. Equally, you will find the videos and CDs listed at the end of the book extremely useful.

You will also be able to think up your own exercises according to your own special interests. Some of you may be particularly drawn to lighting and will find points of reference for your experiments. Others may wish to pursue Wilson's 'magic' tricks with objects, invisible strings and all. My exercises will not cover everything relevant to an imaginary Wilson 'guidebook'. For, if he is a polymath, in general, he is a theatre polymath, in particular, going well beyond my limited selection and the limitations of our task. Yet, whatever elements you choose and however you work with them, whether from within the frames proposed by these exercises or within the parameters that you set yourself, the important thing to remember is this: 'fill the form', as Wilson puts it, with your individual character, qualities and dreams. Fill it with your private, 'interior reflection'. At the same time, have an idea of how the person is working next to you so that you can 'breathe together', as we heard Wilson say during the London rehearsals of *The Black Rider*.

The exercises are flexible. You may work with your class, helped by your teacher, and/or independently with your colleagues and friends outside the class situation. How you group together is bound to be related to the study requirements and resources of your university or other school.

However, one thing is not negotiable, and that is your working space. Prepare it:

- Clean your floors and get rid of the empty paper coffee cups, plastic water bottles and sandwich wrappings that usually tend to litter studios; and take away your own rubbish with you. You need a clean, uncluttered space to concentrate, and to see and to hear what you are doing.
- You need silence for the same reasons unless, of course, talking, music and other sounds are part of the exercise. Do not whisper when you watch people work because this, too, distracts both your attention and the attention of the doers.
- You can wear your usual training clothes, providing that you can move easily in them. On the other hand, you may want to do movement work in a long, loose shift or tunic-style garment: this applies to men as well as women. The slight flow of such clothes will affect the quality of your movement and help you to develop a light step. Preferably wear soft shoes.

MOVEMENT

We know that, for Wilson, all stage elements are of equal importance for the whole composition (see Chapter 2) or what he sometimes calls the 'total stage picture' (Wilson, 1977b: 78). Wilson's account of *I Was Sitting on My Patio*, which he began straight after *Einstein*, is a useful reminder:

> I am always concerned with how the total stage picture looks at any given moment. The placement and design (shape, proportion, materials) of furniture, the colour, fabric and design of costumes, placement and content of film, paths and gestures of performers, and lighting were all major considerations, no less important than the dialog or music.
>
> (Ibid.)

This equal consideration is one major reason why he does not privilege the actor as *the* central power of a performance. We also know that, if Wilson rejects the idea of hierarchies for performance, procedural priorities nevertheless kick-in to his work. He starts thinking about a production with his visual book, and starts staging it with light. We, by contrast, are going to start with movement, which is the underlying principle of everything Wilson does, including paint and shape with light. Movement is the dynamic of his work. There is a second, practical reason for starting with movement. You move with your body, movement is in your body and your body is your instrument, with you all the time. It is most convenient for you to work with what you always have at your disposal.

BREATHING

It is highly advisable to do some breathing exercises to initiate the movement ones. Breath centres your body, relaxes you, facilitates concentration and regulates your pace. It helps you to determine the kind of movement you wish to make as well as to control it. The breathing you do in yoga, Pilates and several of the martial arts is ideal for our purposes. In case you are not familiar with any of these, carry out the following.

Exercise 4.1

➤ Lie flat on the floor with your spine right on it, straight, but not rigid. Your arms are relaxed by your sides. Take a deep breath from below your navel, starting at your pelvic bone. Feel your breath rise right through your body and enter your head. Exhale very slowly through your body. Your mouth is slightly open, but do not push your breath through your mouth. Repeat this 20 times. In the next series of breathings, focus in your mind on a part of your body, say your shoulder, or your elbow, or knee, and exhale *into* that part. Consciously think of it as *sending* your breath into that part. Alternate your breathing into one or two other parts so that you become more aware, with your breath rather than your intellect, of the parts and the whole, as well as of the inhale–exhale rhythm you have established. Do not hurry any stage of your breathing. Take your time and keep it to one, regular tempo and rhythm.

➤ When you have found your breath pattern, add small movements to it. For instance, prepare by taking an in-breath and then, as you slowly exhale, slide your foot up slowly off the floor so that your knee bends. Slide it back to your start position on your next in-breath. Do this ten times, and alternate legs. Then send your arm out to the side with your exhalation and bring it back to your side on your inhalation. Repeat with the other arm. Never strain your shoulder or grip your hand. Everything you do should be harmonious and effortless, and your repetition should have the ease of something done ritually. You are co-ordinating breath, motion, time and rhythm. You may feel like a Wilson trance actor when you are done, but you will not actually go into a trance!

WALKING

Exercise 4.2

➤ Stand up and, keeping the sense of breathing and rhythm that you now have in your body, walk slowly in your natural walk in any direction in the studio. Stick to one direction only. The idea is to carve out your space deliberately and make it look deliberate. Do not make it look random by walking about in different directions. Then walk backwards in the same way, again only in one direction. You may change direction on the next try, but always go on one line.

➤ Be aware of any people walking in the same direction as you, but do not interact with them. The point is for all of you to define your own space. Try and not have more than four people walking at a time so that you do not make the space too busy. As you walk, think of creating a space around you. The more you think of it as *creating* space rather than simply being in it, the more it will feel and look like self-contained space. An observer should be able to discern this about you and, as well, get a palpable sense of constructed lines of space from your movement, individually and as a small group.

➤ Vary your sensation of space. Walk, say, towards the studio wall, thinking of the space between you and it as short. As you walk, imagine that the space at the back of your head is long. Keep straight, but feel – imagine – your head stretching back towards this long space, which is longer than the studio itself. Then feel your head stretching upwards, as if you were being pulled by a string, then your torso, then your legs. You will find your posture subtly adjusting to the sensation of elongated vertical space, and this will prepare your body for the next stage of the exercise.

➤ You are now going to stylise your walk. Prepare to go in the same direction by starting to count '1, 2, 3, 4' very slowly. Your time is that of a semibreve in music, that is, four equal beats to every count: you hold four beats to '1', four to '2' and so on. When you start to walk, lift your right heel to four such slow beats and put your foot down to four beats. As you are doing this, you will shift balance so that you are on the ball of the left foot behind you. Lift your left foot with your knee bent and bring it forward, all to the count of eight. Put your left heel down to four beats, and then step to four while you shift the balance and you are now on the ball of your right foot. Keep repeating until you feel that you are fully immersed in the movement.

➤ Once you have the pace of the walk, add stylised arms to it. Put your right arm forward, slightly curved. Your left arm is very slightly behind you, just enough so that you can still see it with your peripheral vision. Your hands are slightly cupped and yours fingers curved and open. Depress your third finger. Your digit can be slightly higher than your fourth. The aim is to have soft, but sculptured hands – not dead fish. Walk with your arms held in this pose. Do not let them swing. Make sure your head is erect, but not stiff. Your eyes look forward. Never look down to the floor. Your feet have to be absolutely sure of where they are going (which is why you have practised the walk first). Think in terms of time, pace, articulated placing of the feet, posture, the line of your body and your overall hieratic, but certainly not rigid, appearance.

CONTRASTS

When you think you have the appropriate silhouette and are comfortable with it, you can experiment with contrasts.

Exercise 4.3

➤ Try your basic walk to a different count, say, '1, 2'. Your arms can be by your side or in the position of the preceding exercise. Experiment with different tempi for the whole group so that some of you are on '1, 2, 3, 4', while others are on half that time ('1, 2') and still others are on double time ('1' to '8'). Avoid falling into chaos by making sure that everybody is always counting together on '1' (but not aloud!).

This is a wonderful exercise for training concentration and focus: you have to resist distraction from a tempo countering yours. Similarly, you cannot be beaten off your track by someone else's trajectory. If their path looks as if it will cross yours, let it happen, but do not lose your tempo. You may have to slow down your *pace*, but not your time, so as not to crash into each other. This and the next exercise are also wonderful for gauging space: the space as a whole, spatial distance and proximity, and spaces between people. Be constantly aware of how you are tracing lines in space, and how everybody together is designing it. In this way you will *inhabit* your space, which, we have seen, is fundamental for Wilson. Once again, do not make the space too busy. Somebody in your group may wish to observe the patterns and draw the designs on paper.

Exercise 4.4

➤ Bring out the contrasts you have begun to make by accentuating lines of movement. Walk with your arms stylised, as before, rather than hang them beside you. Combine a diagonal line with, say, a horizontal by having two people moving diagonally in one direction and two horizontally in the opposite direction. Try two diagonals that cross. You could have parallel horizontals. You could divide the space between these parallels into two triangles by having several people move diagonally in the same direction. You could divide the entire space into two equal halves by a vertical line, that is, have one person walk from the front of the space in a straight line to the back. You can play with people walking backwards, as Wilson frequently does.

Apart from inhabiting the space that you have determined for yourself, you need to be conscious of how you are dissecting and arranging it, as do painters and dancers. Be as inventive as possible not only in this exercise, but also in all the exercises outlined. You might be surprised to discover just how rich such simple means can be.

Once you have the flow of your walking and its relation to space, introduce a contrast of dynamics by using full stops. However, do not break the flow. Your sensation is that movement and stillness are on the same continuum, as Wilson conceives it.

Exercise 4.5

➤ Walk to the beat of a semibreve first (you can speed up your tempo later) and then freeze your movement. It does not matter where you freeze it. For example, your heel could be up, in mid-movement. The way to achieve the sensation of a continuum is to keep counting the time in your head. Second, keep the stop poised, as if you were about to start again. The same principle holds for when your foot is down rather than in mid-air. In this case, do not put the full weight of your body down on to your foot. Go effortlessly into some stops. Let others happen abruptly. Allow your stillness sometimes to be longer and sometimes shorter. By these means you will syncopate rhythm, but never do it too much. The key to Wilson-style contrasts is in the balance: nothing is overdone; less is more.

➤ Develop this exercise with your arms. Here you can really accentuate your gestures. You could suddenly swing your right arm out, or up, or bent to your opposite shoulder. After some 'trance' walking, just as suddenly swing it back. Think of Childs swinging her arm out in *Einstein on the Beach*. Childs not so much walks there as bounces or prances, and you could transform your basic walk in much the same way. You could, of course, make all your arm movements more dance-like, and this would not only affect your leg movements, but also how you stop.

➤ Now develop the dance-like quality of your whole body. Try flowing quite noticeably into a stop. Hold the pose. Then stand on one leg and put the other to your side with your foot extended, as if you were going to point it. Tilt your body towards your extended foot. As you do this, extend one arm upwards while the other stretches towards the floor. You could hold this – freeze it – for however long suits the atmosphere or feeling of your movement.

➤ Do variations on this theme using arabesque-like positions with one arm lifted and the other out to your side. Or you could have both arms curved upwards, not too high. One of your legs is lifted and straight, or you can lift it bent. Bend your torso towards your lifted arm. When you repeat the movement, bend towards your lifted leg. Be conscious of the line of your body as you execute these movements. The idea of line is as fundamental to dancers and choreographers as it is to Wilson, and you *are* here developing the aspect of dance.

➤ Try the earlier sequence with a partner, who will do the opposite of what you do. Thus, if you are tilting towards your extended foot, your partner should be tilting towards you. His/her extended foot need not be to the side, like yours. This is not a play of mirrors, but of contrasts, so look for the most telling contrasts that you can find.

VARIATIONS

So far, you have essentially been working with what I have called the basic Wilson walk. However, although this measured walk, which originates in his 'silent operas', is a Wilson signature, it is only one of numerous movements that he has explored over the years. When you look at the video, *The Making of a Monologue: Robert Wilson's* Hamlet, you will find a plethora of short, sharp walks, sudden turns, movements in which Wilson's body goes around itself, and those in which he lies down on his side, or on his back, in all kinds of variations on the motif of repose.

Similarly, you will see an exclamatory use of his arms and hands quite different from the curved, sculptured arms and hands of the exercises mentioned earlier. The fingers of Wilson's hands for *Hamlet* are usually extended (but not rigid). He places his hands in a decisive manner, often lifting them at the wrists to draw attention either to the palms or the back of the hands. He extends, lifts and drops his arms in a pronounced way. His pace is quite fast. Gone is the legendary Wilson slowness, in every respect.

Elsewhere he has what Wilson, when rehearsing *The Black Rider*, called the 'bunny run'. This is a light run on the balls of the feet. Then there is Woyzeck's or Peer Gynt's speedy run, and numerous variations on it that are not as energetic. There are heavy treads throughout his productions, and any amount of stepping about on tiptoe, slides, shuffles and jumps. Jumps are usually unexpected and, like Wilson's 'silent scream', can have the effect of a punctuation mark. And there are countless echoes of dance, going from ballet to vaudeville.

You can experiment with any number of movements like these in any combination. The crucial thing, however, is not to make them too expressive either of a character or yourself. Make them technically crisp. Meanwhile, think where you might use them, whether in a silent piece or with texts. Think also of the kinds of emotions suggested by your movements, or of emotions that could be triggered off by them. We could call this 'emotional tone'. Here are a few possibilities.

Exercise 4.6

➤ Take two strides forward ('1, 2'), and on the third beat ('3') push your arms out quite violently with your wrists up.

➤ Take two strides forward. Add a third step on which you do a sharp full turn, ending your turn at the point of departure. Now do this turn quickly, but gently. Now do it slowly and gently. Now do it slowly and heavily.

➤ Do a very short, very light 'bunny run' on any one of the lines you have practised walking (diagonal, and so on). Change the line and do a longer run. Then repeat and repeat it as often as you sense is right for the movement.

➤ Dance waltz steps (or fox trot, or tango, or salsa) with your partner. Dance them facing your partner, but not touching him or her. Dance them as variations, say in the style of jive, then as club dancing. Whichever way you vary the base steps, make sure that they are recognisably waltz, fox trot or tango steps overlaid by another dance genre. Thus you will have a 'jivey' waltz, and so forth.

➤ Chose your movement and end it unexpectedly with a jump. Repeat this movement, now ending it with a 'silent scream'. In both cases, your punctuation mark must be well articulated. Is it a comma, a full stop, or something else again? Ask your observers so as to test whether it was clear.

➤ Repeat your sequence first ending in a jump and then in a silent scream. Your aim now is to mark the *timing* of your punctuation sign. You do this by moving in profile to your audience, whether in a horizontal or a diagonal line, and then turning your head quickly and sharply to your audience as you jump. The same sharp gesture accompanies your 'silent scream'. In both cases your head turns sideways, but the rest of your body faces your initial direction.

The timing practised in the last bit of these variations is a feature of vaudeville and comic silent films, both much appreciated by Wilson. His advice to actors to watch and learn from Charlie Chaplin and Buster Keaton, as noted in Chapter 2, is well worth following.

MOVEMENT SCORE

You now have enough material to compose a movement score, its length depending on the **breath**, **time**, **timing**, **pace**, **rhythm** and **pattern** of the movements you establish. How you combine these features is up to you, but work into your inner thoughts, your '**interior reflection**'.

Everything you have been doing so far is developing your **sense** of what you are doing. It also appeals to the **senses**, mainly, for the moment, to your and your spectators' kinetic and visual senses. You also have enough at your disposal to determine the **quality**, **feel** and discreet emotional **tone** of your individual movements and gestures, as well as the over-arching feel of your movement score. (These and all other terms in bold indicate key Wilson characteristics.)

Exercise 4.7

➤ Compose your score using the features marked in bold and make sure that you treat all your movement and gestures like **dance**, no matter how held-back they might be. Your score is **structured**, **shaped**. It has **line**, **motion** and **sequence** and commands **space**, exactly as happens in a **choreography**. Remember that your score is neither a haphazard nor a mechanical combination, but a choreographed piece. Watch your **posture** and how you **place** your limbs.

BODY IMAGING

Clearly, all your movements create visual images of some sort and, in this sense, everything that not only Wilson does, but that we do, is a matter of images. The distinction that applies to Wilson is the intentional, stylised and highlighted way in which he creates images, drawing your eye to them so that you see their contours in full. We have observed in the preceding chapters how Wilson sculpts his images and throws them into relief – with the help of light, certainly, but also with costumes and objects. Some of the latter are independent of actors, like the toy spaceship in *Einstein*, or the toys in the prelude to *Woyzeck*. Others are connected functionally in some way to actors, like the frog's martini glass or the women's parasols that burst into flame in *Deafman Glance*.

There are hundreds of images that you could invent to accompany the body imaging occurring in your movement score. Let your imagination loose and experiment. The next exercise variations are deliberately restrained. Their emphasis is on how your body imaging structures and alters your movement score rather than on how imaginatively you construct images as such.

Exercise 4.8

➤ Make costumes out of paper (newspaper, crepe paper) and others out of cardboard. Wear them alternately as you perform your movement score. How do they affect the quality of your movement and, therefore, how it looks?

➤ Wear long, loose Chinese sleeves for your movement score. Now perform it with long, light fabric attached to elastics that you are wearing on your wrists. Now perform it in a long gown whose train is as long as you can make. Let your garment lead your movement in each case. For instance, let your long sleeve guide your arm to slow down and flow. Which movements are you less able to do because of a particular garment? Why? How do you handle your train? Do you smooth it out of your way with your feet, when you turn, or do you give it a swift kick?

➤ Choose any costume and wear ballet slippers. Then try trainers, normal flat shoes, stiletto heels, and long and short boots. The greater the contrast, like an elegant gown worn with clod-hopping boots, the more challenging the execution of your movement will be. Perform a score that includes a 'bunny run' and a jump, preferably not one after the other, since this is predictable. Be conscious of how your footwear impacts on your step and gait and determines the overall tone of your movement score.

➤ Wear a range of different masks. You have been fairly imperturbable until now, in the Wilson way. Does a mask give you a greater sense of detachment and distance as you move?

➤ Carry an object – a ball, a balloon, a stick, an open umbrella – as you do your movement score. First use it as a 'still' to convey a dream-like sensation. Then 'animate' it by moving it in some way as you move.

The idea of the last variation is to stimulate your sense of **incongruity**, a major Wilson principle. You can use it as a springboard for developing a wide range of incongruous images. The more unlikely you make your **juxtapositions** of object and movement (or, for that matter, of object, movement and costume), the more incongruous – indeed, **surrealistic** – your whole **image** will be.

Isabelle Huppert in *Orlando*, for instance, lightly rummages in a drawer and pulls out a fish! She pulls it out by its tail, and, without breaking her movement, holds it up for display. It is a totally surrealistic moment and, of course, humorous. Observe how Wilson in the *Hamlet* video moves from a trunk carrying two different shoes. Then observe how he places them in the neck of two costumes, calling them 'Rosencrantz' and 'Guildenstern'. (So both the shoes and the costumes 'represent' the characters.) This moment is also surrealistic and funny. Do not be afraid to play with **humour**, as Wilson is not, much to the consternation of those spectators who expect his work to be solemn because it has been described as 'avant-garde', or 'arty', or 'slow'.

MAKE-UP

You can have enormous fun with make-up, discovering its various effects.

Exercise 4.9

➤ First of all, whiten your face and hands and any other exposed part of your body. Your movement exercises will have helped you to come closer to the impassive 'death-like Beauty' imagined by Craig and realised by Wilson. The whiteness of your body will encourage you to perceive yourself differently. Use it consciously to adopt a persona – not a character, but a performing 'other' who is in you, but is not your daily self or selves ('selves' on the assumption that we are many people at once in everyday life).

Remember that make-up in Wilson's work, white or coloured, is never merely decorative. The whiteness of his actors' faces and bodies, although canvases on which he paints light, have a mask-like effect; and it is integral to the cool **distance** cultivated by his actors from their roles, each other and the spectators.

It is not the whiteness as such, but how you move and behave when covered in whiteness that conveys the otherworldly and, sometimes, completely ethereal impression that spectators receive from such a figure. (It comes from the Western mime tradition via *commedia dell'arte* and from the Eastern Noh and Kabuki traditions, among other Eastern forms. Contemporary Butoh groups like Sankai-Juku whitewash their entire bodies.) Also, your eyes and mouth will need to be accentuated, although how heavily you make them up will depend on what you wish to achieve.

• Think, now, about identifying a character not from the psychological inside, but from the outside of **surface** appearances. Your make-up will provide that surface identification. Say your character falls into the 'vampire' range of characters evident in *The Black Rider*. You could blacken your eyes in circles around them, or extend the black, like a cat-mask, to the edge of your face. You could over-arch your eyebrows and redden – or blacken – your lips, tongue and a tooth or two.

This kind of make-up in *The Black Rider* both enjoys and burlesques standard techniques used in vaudeville, silent films, Gothic horror films, cartoons and comic strips, and contributes quite considerably to the high-camp effects exploited by the production as a whole. Heavy facial make-up need not necessarily be camp. The character you want to identify will determine the way you use it, as will the tone(s) and temper(s) that you find appropriate for your piece.

COMPOSING A SILENT PLAY

You now have all the components required to make an extended piece of work and, as well, you have the sequences that you composed while you were executing some of the exercises. You have been working to silence except, of course, for the extraneous sounds around you. You will have realised that there is no such thing as silence, as John Cage claims; also, that intended silence, the silence that *you* construct, has a concentration and pulse of its own – so much so that it can become palpable, vibrant and draw you into its vortex.

A good deal of the power exerted by silence has to do with your attitude to it, with how focused you are on what you are doing, and with how calmly you project, as if independently of yourself, your attention on your action. This nexus is at the very core of Wilson's silent operas, and is something that he sought afterwards, when his actors began to speak. Words, when he came to use them, were not to override the special quality achieved by means of silence. In order to underscore this special quality (although Wilson is not heavy-handed about it), he inserts cameos of silent play into his drama and opera productions. Their effect in the latter works is like that of scenes in a film where the sound is suddenly cut and everything begins to happen in slow motion.

Exercise 4.10

➤ With all your components in hand, find a theme and build a silent play around it of some duration. Your theme does not have to hold up a story, anymore than did *The Life and Times of Sigmund Freud.* It is merely a starting point. Your play can be a solo or involve various numbers of people. The essential point is that you (singular or plural) be inwardly thoughtful so that you capture the **interiority** of an action as you do it (which is partly what Wilson means when he tells his actors to be 'interior'). Your silent play will benefit if you think of it as a dream play or a silent film – *minus*, however, the exaggerated mimicry and gesticulation of the latter. Let your objects/props and costumes be an integral part of that dream or silent film.

At some point in your various attempts, try and construct a silent play built on multiple rhythms, all going at their own tempo, simultaneously. Think, for example, of *Freud* where a man keeps running across the back of the stage, a tortoise crawls across it at the front, and a chair comes down at another, slower pace still than the tortoise. Your polyrhythmic composition in silence will help to sensitise your ear to polyrhythmic work with sound.

SOUND AND MUSIC

The preceding groups of exercises have enabled you to add components, one after the other, leading you to your silent play. This is the beginning of the kind of **layering** process or structuring on separate tracks that is fundamental to Wilson's aesthetics. Ideally, you have not been layering to blend your elements but to disjoin them, taking care to leave space between them (Wilson's concept of 'track' is especially useful for this idea) so that each one of them can be set off against the next.

You are going to complicate this process by adding a new layer, which is that of sound. When you use sound-other-than-music together *with* music, you should see them as different layers: music, although sonic, is a separate component. The same distinction holds for non-verbal vocal sounds and the sounds of language (speech). So, you will have four separate layers: sound, music, vocalisation ('paralinguistics') and language. The exercises below are divided in this way, but not in this order. You can change the order about to best suit your purposes.

FOUND SOUNDS

It would be interesting to create a sound score for your silent play. Equally, you could set to sound the polyrhythmic experiments that you have done previously, harmonically or contrapuntally. Wilson often speaks of the freedom to be had from adding sounds *mentally* to images – indeed, as you might do when you watch a silent film and imagine a protagonist's voice, or imagine the screech of the wheels of a bus. Similar freedom comes, he maintains, from conjuring up images while you listen to a radio play. His 'ideal theatre would be a cross between the radio play and the silent movie' (Wilson quoted in Teschke, 1999: 11). This indicates why his method, when he develops a production, is to juxtapose the two freedoms so that neither the visual nor the sonic illustrate each other, but maintain their individual strengths.

As you work on the sound scores suggested later, think of them as liberating both your imagination and the imagination of your listeners. (This applies to all the sound exercises and not only to the found sound ones.) Intrigue your listeners. Spark off their capacity to daydream with evocative sounds that they cannot quite pinpoint.

Use different timbres, pitches, volumes, tempi and rhythms. Experiment, as well, with crescendos and diminuendos by increasing the volume as well as gradually decreasing it. Decide on a tempo and rhythm, and maintain them as you regulate your volume. Then try speeding them up or, conversely, slowing them down to various volumes so as to see what sonic effect such conjunctions may have. Compare, say, a very loud high pitch with one that is very high, but soft. Work on the line of the sound, as you have on the line of the body, so that it has a clear, crisp, silhouette.

Exercise 4.11

➤ Collect an array of sounds found in your studio: the rustle of paper, the scrape of a chair, the noise of a window banging shut, and so on. Select and arrange these sounds in a stimulating manner, seeking contrasts that will accentuate the differences between, timbres, pitches and so forth. The whisper of a rustle, for example, could be juxtaposed against a high-pitched scrape.

Be careful not to bunch up too many sounds together. Pace and place them (especially in those spots where you risk losing their individuality) so that your listeners can savour them and fully notice the gaps of silence between them. You could amplify some sounds and feed them into a synthesiser or a computer to alter their quality. All these indications are equally valid for the next exercise.

Exercise 4.12

➤ Record sounds in the streets, at train stations, supermarkets and anywhere else in a daily-life context that you might fancy. Write a score from your selection, but remember that nothing obliges you to stick to this particular range. You could mix sounds from it with items from your preceding score(s) and keep reshuffling the combinations.

Of course, by now, you might be composing quite intricate sound scores for any number of silent plays. You can also think of them as anticipating the addition of music and texts, which you will be doing shortly. What you want at this stage, above all, is to train your ear to be open to sonic possibilities and to develop your capacity for *listening*. These skills will be invaluable when you bring the vocal **sonorities** of language into your scores. And they will be of great benefit for any kind of text-based performance you might care to do, even of the most traditional dialogue-driven type. All too often, we forget that the theatre is not only a place of seeing (*theatron* from which 'theatre' is derived), but a place of *hearing* – something Wilson, in his own particular way, has never ignored. Moreover, hearing/listening is, for Wilson, an alert and completely physical activity:

> My theatre is, in some ways, really closer to animal behaviour. When a dog stalks a bird his whole body is listening (*Performs the dog.*). He's not listening with his ears, with his head; it's the whole body. The eyes are listening.
>
> (Schechner, 2003: 120)

You will certainly have been experimenting with sound equipment, including microphones and loud speakers to amplify sound. Continue your research by having sounds run from various spots in your work-space at various volumes. Have them stop and start abruptly, and come in and out of focus. Have them circle your space, as in the scene in *Peer Gynt* discussed in Chapter 2. When you add sound to your silent play and perform it, remember that the fact of its coming from a direction different to the direction of your gaze opens up the spaces around the sound. It also opens up the view for your spectators. In this way, their visual and aural perception is altered.

The **spatialisation** of sound – its 360-degree radius – is quintessentially 'Wilson', and his interest in the three-dimensional quality of sound developed, as we have noted, through his collaboration with Hans Peter Kuhn. You could work in a similarly highly productive way with a collaborator, transferring the responsibility of sound to him/her while you concentrate on another aspect of your work together.

NATURAL SOUNDS

Wilson heightens the sounds of nature so as to break with naturalistic conventions and accentuate how, on the stage, these sounds are artificial. We have seen that, for him, artifice is the necessary condition of the theatre. Nevertheless, these 'doctored' sounds can recognisably be *from* nature, as is true of the crashing waves of the sea that come from the back of the auditorium in *Peer Gynt*. The same is true of the waves that erupt unexpectedly in the soundscape of *La Maladie de la mort*. Sea sounds in *Peer Gynt* accord with the narrative, but they seem quite arbitrary in *La Maladie* (until you go back to the text by Marguerite Duras and realise that the sea is one of her central tropes). Either way, they are exaggerated sounds, and sounds that are amplified to such a degree that they begin to lose their natural quality. The human-made, technological intervention in the process distances them from their natural source, thus helping to make them artificial sounds of the theatre.

Exercise 4.13

➤ Record natural sounds – the wind, rain, a babbling brook – and amplify them or interfere in their transmission in such a way that you estrange them from their origins. Layer them into your found sounds or into the animal and language sounds explored in the exercises mentioned later. Your aim is to establish **textures** of sound.

ANIMAL SOUNDS

Wilson generally uses animal sounds playfully. More often than not, actors make them for comic effect. Sometimes the actors create a sound fantasia for their designated animal, like the actor playing a monkey in Act IV of *Peer Gynt*. The spectators hear fabulous, melodic chuckles and chortles coming from the flies well before they see a white rope drop. As the rope falls lower, a white rope ladder appears carrying an actor in a suit rather reminiscent of the bellboy suits-with-cap worn by monkeys in 1940s Hollywood movies. The white rope is the monkey's tale. The actor's make-up – white face and eyes circled in black – completes the humorous impersonation. The fact that the spectators hear the sounds before they realise who or what is producing them adds to the fun of the scene.

At other times, the actors' meows, squeaks, growls and so forth are doubled by a pre-recording of the same sounds. These are powerfully amplified a split second behind the actors' emission of them. Such is the case, for instance, of the lion in *Les Fables de la Fonataine*. The contrived echo of the actor's roar gives the sound **resonance** and makes it **reverberate** in space. It also enlarges the actor's already excessive imitation of a lion, in which he delights knowingly, like a child playing a game at 'being' a lion.

Now and then, recorded animal sounds substitute actors and are associated with the characters and the situations that they are playing. This happens in the opening scene of Act IV of *The Winter's Tale*. Here the ba-ba of sheep precedes the entry of Perdita, a shepherdess, who does not know that she is a princess, and Florizel, a prince disguised as a shepherd. Shortly after the sound is heard, small, mechanised sheep appear, seemingly gambling over 'hills' against a night sky dotted with stars and stretching to a faintly illuminated horizon. The 'hills' are a low, three-tiered platform the length of the stage, which, with the 'sky', give the illusion of open space. It is an event from a picture book or a fairy tale, and is all the more child-like for the continuous 'ba-ba' spatialised throughout the auditorium. This is another example of the disparity discussed earlier between where your view is directed and the direction from which sound comes.

Exercise 4.14

➤ Collect a range of different animal sounds. You can record them, but also learn to do them yourself. Then take a range within one species, say, birds, and explore their differences – the cackle of geese, the hoot of owls, the twitter of sparrows, all of which you can intimate or fully articulate, soft as well as loud, high and low, and all the gradations in between. You and your colleagues can have a veritable animal symphony! Practise your animal sounds and look for the resonators in your body through which to produce them. Produce sounds from deep within your belly, shift them towards your back, and lift them into your head so that a high-pitched sound comes through its very crown. The idea is to learn how to make your body like a resonating chamber and, as well, to isolate resonating body parts. The breathing exercises noted at the very beginning of this chapter will help you to achieve both.

➤ Take a group of fables either by La Fontaine or Aesop (whom you may have read as a child) and find appropriate sound images for the animals speaking in them. Try and construct concise animal-sound poems that clinch the fables' meaning, like haiku.

PARALINGUISTIC EFFECTS

In the preceding exercise, you began the work required for making vocal sounds that are not words. Wilson's productions have a whole arsenal of such paralinguistic effects: yelps, yowls, grunts, moans, whisperings, stutters, sibilants, fricatives and more, which make different demands on the vocal chords, the air passages of the noise and the projection of the mouth. Usually, the actors directed by Wilson produce these effects in a relatively deadpan manner, unless his aim is to camp them up for ironic, mock-heroic or otherwise burlesque purposes. The sounds at issue may or may not belong to a character. They may simply ornament his or her voice, like grace notes in music. But whether they help to identify a character or not, they invariably contribute to a given sound score's texture and density, which, although features of composition, as they are in music, are integral to the **mood** and **atmosphere** that sounds help to create.

It is important to remember that Wilson frequently overlays found or natural sounds with paralinguistic effects. Thus the screech of birds in a forest scene in *The Black Rider* is overlaid by strangely indeterminate crackles that evoke a supernatural world. The composition is appropriate for the production's demonic subject and establishes the nocturnal, sinister atmosphere of the scene in question. Wilson's visual structure – oblique lighting, shadows, dark figures with outsize birds' heads, screens and scrims – is also instrumental in creating this atmosphere. At the same time, it throws the sound structure into relief. You may decide not to overlay sounds in this way, let alone to set them off against any visual effects, until you are ready to tell a story, whether it is a silent play, spoken or sung.

Exercise 4.15

➤ Make paralinguistic sounds spontaneously to free yourself of any inhibitions.

➤ Practise resonating the different parts of your body and filling your body with these sounds.

➤ Experiment with creating moods and atmospheres with combinations of paralinguistic effects. It can help to think of your sounds as emotions and to vocalise them as such (pain, fear, excitement, foreboding – find your own keys). Practise them in a variety of ways to see how such sounds acquire different colourings through different intonations.

LETTERS AND WORDS

Give your imagination free reign.

Exercise 4.16

➤ Play with letters, vowels, consonants and words. Play with phonetics and intonations. Cool them, heat them. Laugh, shout and scream them. Sob and purr them. Let them **vibrate** in your body and reverberate. Take them deep into your chest, stomach and bottom. Send them out, as far away from you as you can. Avoid scrunching them up. Give them space. Roll your 'r's, hiss your 's's, titillate your 't's and dig your 'd's. You might want to prolong the first letter of a word ('sssssssss' of 'snake'), or accentuate the vowels or consonants that constitute a word ('s-n-ake'). You could pronounce and overpronounce them. Isolate them. You could construct whole dialogues out of syllables, as did Wilson and Knowles in *A Letter for Queen Victoria*. Speak and sing nonsense rhymes and sentences, and accentuate the sonorities of your invented words. Articulate real words and savour their taste in your mouth. Repeat and repeat them, listening to their beat, phrasing and cadences. Say them in a flat, monotonous way.

MUSIC

There is an infinite number of ways of using music in the theatre. We are well aware that music expresses and induces mood; that it stimulates our bodies and emotions; that it helps our minds to relax. Wilson frequently uses music in his first workshop with actors, when they learn movement scores before texts are added to the process. Music helps them to release their tensions as well as to find their internal rhythm. It is a valuable support for Wilson in his search for the right moods for the episodes of his planned production, irrespective of whether he ends up using music for them or not. The music leaves traces in his conscious and unconscious mind, and he is able to convey its mood through other media like movement, colour or light. His principle of running material on separate tracks ensures that music neither illustrates nor merely repeats what is 'said' by other means on the stage, but is in a dynamic **counterpoint** to the rest. This is especially noticeable when he stages opera, where he avoids any kind of redundancy. The singers' acting is cool, whereas their voices carry the relevant 'hot' emotion. Their movement is composed, whereas the orchestra expresses the drama of the music.

Work, first, *with* whatever music you choose from whichever range – club, blues, heavy metal, classical – rather than in counterpoint to it. Dance and sing to its rhythms. This will help your body to feel the difference when you work independently of it.

Exercise 4.17

➤   Chose a piece of music, or make an **assemblage** or a **collage** from various pieces of music, and add it to the movement and sound scores that you have in your repertoire. Make sure that you (singular or plural) are not tempted to sway to the rhythm of the music, or to tap your feet in time. If you do this, you will reiterate what the music is already doing. Where your sound scores are concerned, avoid loud, aggressive music, for example, if you have strong found or animal sounds.

This exercise is not a pretext for cacophony. It requires a good deal of acumen in your choice of music so that, although not in line with everything else that you establish, it actually 'fits'. Counterpoint in music is not a matter of chaos, anymore than it is in dance, as Cunningham has demonstrated. Look at Wilson's *Hamlet* video and notice how the production's synthesised music goes well with its other elements, including Wilson's performance. None of them are really generically alike, and yet the whole is anything but an indiscriminate jumble.

- Try using the recordings of *Einstein on the Beach*, *The Black Rider* and *Blood Money* (see the discography) for the body imaging that you have been practising. Then make new body images while listening to the recordings. When you do this, keep in mind that you will be working with texts later on.

Waits's songs have texts. Do they affect your physical imagery? Are you tempted to 'translate' the songs in image terms (rather like your hand to your heart to say 'I love you')? How would you avoid gestures as literal as this and find images involving your whole body that are **elliptical** and poetic rather than a matter of flat statement?

- Suddenly stop the music and continue your action without it so that the interruption or pause is understood to be a component of your sound structure. How does the counterpoint of sound to silence affect your body imaging? Keep practising this type of counterpoint until you feel that you have an unbroken flow of imaging which links sound to silence in one continuum.

It is difficult to formalise movement to music that wants to sweep you along with it, especially when it has lyrics that push you in its direction, as well. This is one of many reasons why Wilson has actors and opera singers move to a precise count. Moving to the count of '1, 2, 3, 4' and so on, inculcates a sense of form in them, regardless of the music's emotional pulse. Your task is to learn to counter your spontaneous response to the melody and harmony of music, which, for most people, usually means humming its tune.

Wilson held a workshop on Bizet's opera *Carmen* at Watermill in 2002 where the actors walked on to the stage, one after another at precise intervals, to counts relayed to them through a microphone. The scene was one of the opening scenes involving a chorus. Clearly, Wilson wanted his chorus to follow the underlying tempo of the music and thus to adhere to its form rather than be led by its vocal and orchestral force.

Exercise 4.18

➤ You could take chorus pieces from *Carmen* and imitate Wilson's method, making sure that one of your group counts loudly for all to hear.

➤ It would be even more challenging to apply this counting method to such very well-known arias from *Carmen* as the 'Habanera' and 'Toreador' arias. You would have to work really hard counter-intuitively against their rhythmic and melodic drive. Walking quite precisely to a mathematical count, with each one of you entering on a different number, would curtail your temptation to hum the melodies, sing along with the music, sway with it, or tap your hands or feet! The fact that you all enter on a different number (Rachel on '3', Simon on '7', Anna on '10' and so forth) does not necessarily mean that everyone stops moving once they are on the stage. It is up to you to see what offers the most arresting combination of movement and non-movement, which is like a mirror exercise of the counterpoint of sound to silence that you have been mastering.

WORKING WITH TEXTS

VISUAL BOOK

How Wilson came about his visual-book method is a matter of conjecture, but it is an efficient means of keeping the idea of drama as literature at bay. Similarly, it is instrumental in his efforts to avoid interpretation, especially of the psychological, cause-and-effect kind that he equates with 'naturalism'. We have also observed that he admits to 'interpretation' in so far as the term applies to what could be called his 'approach' or 'take' on a particular subject as *embodied* in a production. He resists, however, the idea of 'interpretation' as 'having a fixed idea' about something. Wilson's visual book is not the outcome of textual analysis, but of the sensations and impressions derived by him pictorially from the retelling of a text by his dramaturgs.

We must also remember that, until the early 1980s, Wilson and his co-performers wrote their own texts, either wholly (*Queen Victoria*) or partly (*Einstein*). And there were the two-handers for Wilson and Knowles and Wilson and Childs, as noted in Chapter 1, which were similarly built on word and sound patterns rather than on semantic meanings.

Wilson must surely have honed his visual-book method on these early, 'abstract' writings. The skill for visual synopsis that he gradually perfected served him well when it came to extrapolating essential points from verbally meaningful texts. His is an idiosyncratic approach, and you may not like drawing. Nevertheless, try the exercise that follows to see how his process of visualisation might operate.

Exercise 4.19

➤ Write your own text and divide it into episodes, scenes or sequences as you draw and imagine how you might organise your space. As you sketch, think where you might have a screen or a drop, and whether you would run a film at some point, or show slides. How would such visual overlay affect your spatial structure? Would you use any décor and how would it affect your space? How would you co-ordinate your script with your pictures, but not have one illustrate the other?

➤ Form collaborative groups and brainstorm one of your favourite plays. Several of you can draw a visual book while you all ask questions regarding form comparable to the ones mentioned earlier. It is necessary, as well, to ask questions of substance concerning time, place, narrative, events, numbers of characters, what they are doing and how they relate to each other. Keep it simple. If you have too many factors going at once, you will find sketching the scenes very difficult.

DRAMATURGICAL INTERVENTION

Summaries of a given text complement a visual book, and it is important to remember that Wilson invented the visual book as an antidote to the way theatre directors had privileged texts, downgrading all the other elements that rightfully made up a stage ensemble or *mise en scène*. Wilson's approach to text might be idiosyncratic, but he is not the only director who directs radically abridged and re-organised pre-existing texts, whether they have great status or are less well known. Cutting texts for staging purposes can be a contentious issue. You have heard these objections: the cut text is 'not what the author wrote', 'not what the author intended', and similar complaints. But Wilson is an easier target for critique than most because, in addition, he deviates from the established practices of dramatic theatre (believable characters and motivations behind their actions, among other familiar features).

Even so, there is nothing arbitrary about the textual cuts and reshuffles of Wilson's dramaturgs and to which he might add or subtract bits of text as his productions evolve. It would be wise to remember this as you adopt the role of a dramaturg. Seriously consider what you are cutting away from a well-known play and why you are doing it. Wilson does not doubt, any more than do his dramaturgs, that excisions must have a justification as regards the proposed stage work. All serious dramaturgs proceed according to this principle. However, those who collaborate with Wilson know that they are operating within a very particular, extrapolative style of presentation. I have called it 'imagistic', and it could also be described as a presentation of quintessences. Wilson does not reserve this method for celebrated texts by other people, but treats his own in the same way.

Wilson, we have seen, examines a play's or an opera's narrative backbone before he lifts out what might be quintessential about that play or opera; and its main story guides him to its philosophical content. The story as such and the ideas and issues embedded in it are very much the dramaturg's business, shared with Wilson so that he can conceive the staging. It is up to you to decide whether you want to imitate his collaborators' approach. This would involve talking your way through a play with a colleague, who would envisage a *mise en scène* either in the form of a visual book or simply in words. If you do a visual book, you could add the written synopses to your drawings. This dramaturgical work does not necessarily have to be done in pairs. You could work on your own, writing synopses and then cutting back the dialogue to get to its kernel. Do not forget that your focus here is the *text*, not scenic presentation.

Let us take a straightforward example from *Peer Gynt*. Keep in mind that Monica Ohlsson's dramaturgy is fundamentally concerned with the play's plot sequence, although this is not detrimental to the play's sense. Her edited text, then, is not in the style close to collage-montage employed by Wolfgang Wiens for Wilson's production of *Hamlet*.

The example is the first scene of Act IV. Peer has become rich and brags about his achievements to four other traders with whom he has just had a meal. (The scene that follows is Peer's long monologue about his ship, which was stolen by these men. See Chapter 2 for Wilson's imagistic treatment of it.) I am not quoting the translation into English of the New Norwegian text used for the production since it differs, in terms of choice of words, from the one I have already referred to in this book. Nevertheless, I am able to convey with the latter the *substance* of what was kept and what deleted from Ibsen's play. It is neither the quality of translations nor their variants that interest us, but the excisions made to the text and the reasons for them. The bold typeface denotes the dialogue cut for Wilson's purposes.

Here is the scene at the moment when the discussion moves away from how Peer made his fortune to his underlying ambition:

COTTON:	Yes, but no one hoists his sails just for the love of sailing; /you have a goal, or I'm mistaken.
	You want to be a – ?
PEER GYNT:	An Emperor.
ALL FOUR:	What?
PEER GYNT [*NODDING*]:	Emperor.
ALL:	Of – ?
PEER GYNT:	– All the world!
BALLON:	But how, my friend?
PEER GYNT:	By force of money!
PEER GYNT:	It's by no means a new idea, /it's been the core of all my dealings.
	When young, I used to dream of roving/ high as a cloud across the seas;
	I soared with cloak and gilded blade – / and landed on all fours again.
	But, friends, my goal remained the same. Someone has said – or is it written/ somewhere I don't remember where, that if you conquer all the world/yet lose your Self, all that you gain is a wreath around your broken skull **[– or words to that effect. That text is by no means poetic nonsense.]**
VON EBERKOPF:	But just what *is* the Gyntish Self?
PEER GYNT:	That world inside my vaulted skull/ which makes me *Me* and no one else … just as a god can't be a devil.

TRUMPETERSTRALER:	Ah, now I gather what your aim is.
BALLON:	A great conception!
VON EBERKOPF:	Most poetic!
PEER GYNT [*WITH RISING EXCITEMENT*]:	The Gyntish Self...it is a host/of appetites, desires, and wishes; /**[the Gyntish Self – it is a sea/of fantasies, cravings and demands; in short]** – what stirs inside *my* breast/ and makes me live my life as Me.

[But as the Lord has need of clay/to make a world He can be God in, /so I, in turn, require some gold/to make myself an Emperor.]

(Ibsen, 1980: 113–15)

You can see that the cuts are to Peer's speeches, many of which are much longer elsewhere in Ibsen's text as well as in the New Norwegian; and Ohlsson also abridges most of them, sometimes quite heavily. Yet she keeps what is essential for understanding the actual event (a successful Peer in discussion with four businessmen), the philosophical question that emerges from the dialogue as to what constitutes a self, and the information it communicates regarding Peer's self-centredness (the 'Gyntish' self). All this is fundamental to the play as a whole. The deleted lines, in Ohlsson's view, were superfluous to the main points.

Now let us take an example from Act I of *The Winter's Tale*. Act I is in two scenes, but Wilson's dramaturg, Jutta Febers, cut the first scene out altogether. In it Camillo and Archidamus speak of the great friendship between Leontes and Polixenes, who has been staying with Leontes. Febers goes straight to scene ii so as to focus on the turning point of the plot. Polixines says he must leave. Leontes tries to persuade him to prolong his visit. The production, then, starts with the moment that triggers off the sequence of events of the entire play. Thus:

POLIXENES:	No longer stay.
LEONTES:	One seve'night longer.
POLIXENES:	Very sooth, tomorrow.
LEONTES:	We'll part the time between's then: and in that I'll no gainsaying.

POLIXENES: Press me not, beseech you, so.

[There is not tongue that moves, none, none in the world,
So soon as yours, could win me: so it should now,
Were there necessity in your request, although
'Twere needful I denied it.] My affairs

Do even drag me homeward: which to hinder
Were (in your love) a whip to me; my stay,
To you a charge and trouble: to save both,
Farewell, our brother.

[LEONTES: Tongue-tied our queen? Speak you.

HERMIONE: I had thought, sir, to have held my peace until
You had drawn oaths from him to stay.] You sir,

Charge him too coldly. Tell him you are sure
All in Bohemia's well: this satisfaction
The by-gone day proclaim'd: say this to him,
He's beat from his best ward.

(Shakespeare, 2005: 6–7)

Look at the beginning of Shakespeare's text for comparison and you will see that the text of the production begins quite abruptly: there is no first scene, which Shakespeare uses by way of a prologue, to pave the way. Furthermore, the dialogue between Leontes and Polixenes begins midstream. The dramaturg cuts to the chase, and this entails removing Polixenes's expression of loving friendship to Leontes ('There is no tongue . . .'). It also entails introducing Hermione, Leontes's wife, very quickly into the stage action. This is important because Shakespeare soon shows how violently Leontes reacts to Hermione's influence on Polixenes, suspecting her of infidelity. Leontes denounces Hermione to his faithful follower, Camillo.

A small part of the interchange between Leontes and Camillo provides us with another example of dramaturgical intervention:

LEONTES: Ha' not you seen, Camillo ?

(But that's past doubt: you have, or your eye-glass
Is thicker than a cuckold's horn) or heard?

[[(For to a vision so apparent rumour
Cannot be mute) or thought? (for cogitation
Resides not in that man that does not think)]

My wife is slippery? If thou wilt confess,

> Or else be impudently negative,
> To have not eyes, nor ears, nor thought, then say
> My wife's a hobby-horse, **[deserves a name**
> **As rank as any flax-wench that puts to**
> **Before her troth-plight:]** say't and justify't!

CAMILLO: **[I would not be a stander-by, to hear**
> **My sovereign mistress clouded so, without**
> **My present vengeance taken: 'shrew my heart,]**
> You never spoke what did become you less
> Than this: which to reiterate were sin
> As deep as that, though true.

(Shakespeare, 2005: 20–1)

It is clear that the cuts here moderate both Leontes's vituperations and Camillo's outrage, thereby also reducing the moral, psychological and emotional complexities within Shakespeare's verse. Of course, this procedure dilutes the richness of Shakespeare's language, but it is adapted to Wilson's streamlined style. The dramaturg also pares down, in a similar way, the psycho-emotional scale of the remainder of Act I. The Act ends with Camillo's decision to go into exile and leave Leontes's kingdom with Polixenes. You know the rest of the play.

Exercise 4.20

➤ Take Act I of *The Winter's Tale* and abridge it according to your requirements. See whether you should cut any of scene i, or whether you need it at all. Proceed through what could be called the 'micro-scenes' that make up scene ii. Decide what you think is of central importance to each one, then cut away the 'fat' from its heart. Ask yourself how many cuts are too many. If you have damaged the heart, and thus damaged or destroyed the sense of the dialogue, add lines back in. Always be aware of what your are cutting out and why you are doing it.

➤ Take any canonical play of interest to you, then an established contemporary one, then a recent one that has not made its mark yet, and then one written by you or a friend. The idea is to take a range of plays that will pose quite different editing problems. Choose manageable pieces of text and proceed in much the same way as before.

The next exercise is really a continuation of the preceding one except for the fact that you will now abridge for the purposes of a one-man or a one-woman show. This makes it much harder. Look at the video of Wilson's *Hamlet*. It does not give you the whole of the performance, but you can deduce from some of it how Wiens cut and collated dialogue so that Hamlet's thoughts and speech could remain the focus of the piece.

Exercise 4.21

➤ Choose one Act of *Hamlet* and read it carefully to see how your text could concentrate on Hamlet. Select lines that indicate most clearly Hamlet's perception of, and attitude towards, other characters. This will allow you to reduce the length and the number of responses he makes to them. It will also help you to see which characters, if any, you might delete from the Act so as to keep your focus on Hamlet.

➤ Construct a monologue for Ophelia from her various lines throughout the play. Your aim is to chart Ophelia's relationship with both Hamlet and Polonius and show, as you do this, the sequence of events leading to her death. Be sure that you present the sequence from her words, and thus from her point of view.

IMAGING THE TEXT

'Imaging' is not Wilson's term, but mine to convey two things: how movement and gestures are shaped and stylised through the body (the 'body imaging' referred to earlier in this chapter); how textual extrapolation finds expression visually, kinetically and in terms of colour, 'saying' what is said or implied by the word on the page, but is not necessarily said in the dialogue on the stage (discussed in Chapter 2). We saw, for example, how Woyzeck's running on the spot crystallised something important about the character, as can be gleaned from Büchner's text. At the same time, it communicated something vital to the production both in terms of its text (words and songs combined) and its overall impact. Impact works **subliminally** in Wilson's *oeuvre*, and is part of the imaging process itself.

Exercise 4.22

> ➤ You could start with *The Winter's Tale*, since you have been working on this text. Find an image that articulates something important about the three characters in the opening of scene ii, as quoted earlier. It can be a design image, a movement image or a choice of colour – or all three at once if you can synthesise your ideas in this way.

The purpose is to image what you gather about the characters from the text. You do not have to confine your thinking to this micro-scene alone. You could, for example, refer to the second fragment quoted earlier and re-read the first in its light. Your image might focus on Leontes's friendship with Polixenes, or on his jealousy. You could image a busy Polixenes ('My affairs/Do even drag me homeward'), or Hermione 'tongue-tied'.

- Deepen your understanding of how the adjective applies to Hermione in the context of the play as a whole. Think of how 'tongue-tied' she becomes for 16 years, pretending to be dead until Perdita is found. Take into account, also, that she first re-appears as a statue, silent – 'tongue-tied' in another way. Your images would have to be **concise** and **exact** to be appropriate, otherwise you run the risk of being trivial, as Wilson sometimes does.
- Take a piece that you find particularly striking from *Hamlet*. Work on the situations and the time-and-place contexts in which the characters act. If you take, say, the dialogue between Polonius and Gertrude in Gertrude's chambers, you will need to find an image that crystallises the time, place and situation in an **abstract, non-naturalistic** way. So, you will not want bedroom furniture!

To help you in this exercise, look at how the abstract slabs of rock in the *Hamlet* video capture the idea of a castle. Or how the trunk from which Wilson/Hamlet pulls out shoes, calling them 'Rozencrantz' and 'Guildenstern', tells you about the sea voyage undertaken at Claudius's command to have Hamlet murdered in England. The text of the production omits Claudius's speeches to this effect. Spectators may not grasp Wilson's **allusion** to this precise point in Shakespeare's text, any more than they may 'get' the many visual allusions to Einstein in *Einstein on the Beach*. Yet the performances can be experienced meaningfully without these connections.

LIGHT

We know that light is crucial for Wilson's work and is part of the conception of a piece from the very beginning. It is never applied at a later stage of the production process, let alone at the end, as frequently happens in the theatre. Given light's primary importance, you may be surprised to find that I accord little space to it in this chapter. However, since there is such richness of detail regarding light elsewhere in this book, particularly in Chapter 3, it would be appropriate for you to go back and devise your own approach, artistically speaking, from these details. On the other hand, technically speaking, you will probably need the guidance of technicians and/or light designers, especially of those with a sound knowledge of electronic lighting boards. They will help you with gels, cues, spotlighting, and the various other techniques required to light any show, let alone one that may aspire to the complexities and nuances of Wilson's light design.

Given here are a few simple suggestions for what you might want to do with light.

Exercise 4.23

➤ Create various moods and atmospheres. Observe what your variations do to the space, and whether the space appears to shrink or expand because of how you light it. Imagine scenarios for your moods.

➤ Light scenes (silent or spoken) performed by your colleagues, giving them appropriate atmospheres. Play with cues to see how you can introduce subtleties of light and shade relevant to these performances.

➤ Break your playing space into different areas of light. See if you can paint them in colour, and observe how blocs of colour change the sensation you have of them.

➤ Seek colours that create a sense of energy and dynamism and then light some of the movement scores that you have devised earlier with them.

➤ Experiment with colours that might say something about a character's emotions. This does not have to be text-based. Your characters can be figures in dance movement.

➤ Spotlight figures in your space. Then spotlight separate parts of their body. Do this against the dark, then against various degrees of light that illuminate your playing space, and then against a canvas of light–colour.

You can play with lighting as exercises in themselves so as to learn how to handle the equipment and to master techniques. But you can also see that this whole chapter has taken a cumulative approach, guiding you through a number of steps that can lead you to a complete piece of work. Now that you have followed those steps, you can reverse the order and *start* with light, imagining all the other elements that you have worked in relation to it. Light, then, will be an integral part of the conception of your piece, from the beginning.

A SHORT GLOSSARY
OF TERMS

Abstract Expressionism   A form of non-figurative painting emerging in New York in the 1940s and reaching its peak by the mid-1950s. It was characterised as 'expressionist' by analogy with **German Expressionism** because of its free expression of the painter's innermost emotions and highly personal sense of things, usually conveyed through the movement of vivid colour on the canvas. It paid attention to the sensuous quality of the materials used by the painter. Essentially unrestrained, even exhibitionistic, its name was applied to comparable types of dance and theatre.

Bauhaus   A school founded in 1919 in Weimar, Germany, by the renowned architect Walter Gropius. It was a hotbed of experimentation and innovation in the visual and plastic arts, including architecture, movement and design, which also involved typographical design and the design of furniture and other household goods. It focused on the interrelationship between space, form, shape, colour and material, embracing, also, new industrial materials such as plastic. Its teacher-practitioners were committed to the idea that a renewed way of doing art adequate to modern times would change people's relation to the everyday life. The school was dissolved by the Nazi regime in 1933.

Constructivism   The name is applied to a wide range of approaches to art, those in Soviet Russia differing from their Western European counterpart on issues to do with politics. In Russia during the 1920s, the apogee of Constructivism, the emphasis was placed on the social and, especially, utilitarian function of art rather than on its aesthetic appeal. Regardless of their variety, these approaches have in common the principle of conscious and deliberate composition ('construction') and reliance on geometric arrangement. This tendency was prevalent in set designs of the theatre and the cinema, and became evident in certain choreographies in Europe in the late 1920s and early 1930s, where it merged with aspects of Expressionism. In Russia, it influenced the anti-illusionistic, angular style of acting developed, notably, by Meyerhold.

Cubism   A movement lasting from about 1906 to 1920 and predominantly involving painting and sculpture, it breaks down figures and objects into different planes so as to capture their solid, tangible reality. It is also concerned with how the eye perceives such matter from multiple angles of vision.

Dada   The principal manifestations of Dada, a term coined by the writer Tristan Tzara, appeared in Zürich, Paris, Berlin and New York during the First World War. Dada involved writers, poets, artists, musicians and what today would be called performance artists. It is not a unified movement, and is best described as an attitude. Its iconoclastic, carnivalesque and anarchist view of established and establishment values originated in the disgust of its adherents towards the beliefs and power structures that had fostered the War.

German Expressionism   Expressionists were engaged in painting, literature, film and dance (which came to be known as *Ausdruckstanz*) and focused on their intensely felt subjective experiences of the social world. This self-expression in the case of dance meant liberating the body from the strictures of classical ballet and of social convention regarding physicality. In the case of painting, literature and film, it frequently gave rise to grotesque images, which reflected the creator's critical viewpoint of his/her subject. In film design, it acquired the geometric structures familiar to **Constructivism**. Cabaret was considered to be part of it. Expressionism was allegedly born in reaction to Germany's defeat and humiliation in the First World War and to the country's subsequent economic decline. Flourishing in the 1920s, it was suppressed during the Nazi period for its supposed 'degeneration', but re-emerged in the 1950s, transmuting into a version of **Abstract Expressionism**.

Minimalism   The term is used for a tendency that arose chiefly in the United States in the 1950s and which, by the end of the 1960s, covered a great diversity of styles and concepts. Perhaps one of its defining characteristics is its low content, which means that the subject of, say, a painting or a dance is the painting or the dance itself. In general, it favours the idea of ordinary objects as art, extreme simplicity, repetition or slight ('minimal') variations of the base elements of a composition and, in painting, a 'holistic' approach by which the parts of a composition are together, but not internally related. In music, it eschews the principles of harmony for those of addition, return and sequence.

Modernism   There is little agreement about the meaning of this term and its chronological boundaries. The broad consensus sees the start of modernism around 1885, although when it ends is not so clear. For some, closure occurs in the mid-1930s. For others, modernism continues until the 1960s. Whichever way it is looked at, modernism is related to modernity, to the idea that the latter signifies a radical paradigm shift in all aspects of society. When its social dimension is linked to modernism in this way, modernism is nothing less than a new culture in its entirety. In the more restricted application of the term to the arts and literature, 'modernism' points to the procedures of composition self-consciously and sensuously displayed as *art*. All the movements here cited, arguably including **Minimalism** (at least in its 1950s stage) and excluding **postmodernism**, are integral to modernism.

Postmodernism   Generally linked to late capitalism, or postmodernity, dating from the 1970s, postmodernism is a broadly cultural phenomenon. Originally used in the mid-1970s to identify the pastiche-like and eclectic qualities of contemporary architecture, the word soon gained currency, referring to all areas of cultural production and negating the very idea of art as such. It is the latter which essentially distinguishes it from modernism. Although against the notion of aesthetics as such, it is nevertheless best described as a style whose characteristics are parody, pastiche, fragmentation, discontinuity, disharmony and eclecticism (multiple elements borrowed simultaneously and used at a second degree, as if put in quotation marks). It is anti-realist in so far as it rejects all features associated with realism, including the idea that a work is a coherent, unified totality. In philosophical terms, 'postmodernism' stands, above all, for relativism (thus it rejects the notion of 'truth' as an absolute category) and against faith in explanatory grand schemas (the so-called 'master narratives', including those that ascribe continuity and an end-purpose to history conceived as 'History').

Surrealism   Covering novels, poetry and other writing, including philosophy and 'automatic' writing, which, it claimed, was commanded by subconscious thought, Surrealism also embraced the visual and plastic arts as well as the theatre (thus Artaud). Predominantly a 1920s phenomenon, it lasted into the 1950s in some fields, like painting and the theatre. Concentrated in France, not all of its practitioners were French. Surrealism extolled the virtues of instinct, spontaneity and the world of dreams and desires, which it opposed to reason and rationalism. Most of its creators lay great store by Freud's theories of the unconscious. Some were committed to a utopian conception of communism. Although diverse in its manifestations, the movement aspired to a kind of transcendence – political, psychoanalytical or metaphysical – of immediate, empirically knowable reality. Hence the idea of something above and beyond ('*sur*') the 'real'.

BIBLIOGRAPHY

Appia, Adolphe (1993) *Adolphe Appia: Texts on Theatre*, ed. Richard C. Beacham, London: Routledge

Aragon, Louis (1971) 'Lettre Ouverte à André Breton sur *Le Regard du Sourd: l'art, la science et la liberté*', *Lettres Françaises*, 2–8 June, pp. 3 and 15

Arens, Katherine (1991) 'Robert Wilson: Is Postmodern Performance Possible?', *Theatre Journal* 43: 1, pp. 14–40

Aronson, Arnold (2000a) 'American Theatre in Context: 1945– Present' in *The Cambridge History of American Theatre, Volume Three: Post-World War II to the 1990s*, ed. Don B. Wilmeth and Christopher Bigsby, Cambridge: Cambridge University Press, pp. 87–162

—— (2000b) *American Avant-Garde Theatre: A History*, London: Routledge

Banes, Sally (1987) *Terpischore in Sneakers: Post-modern Dance*, Connecticut: Weslyan University Press

—— (1998) *Subversive Expectations: Performance Art and Paratheater in New York, 1976–85*, Ann Arbor, MI: University of Michigan Press

Brecht, Stefan (1994) *The Theatre of Visions: Robert Wilson*, London: Methuen

Buckle, Richard and John Taras (1988) *George Balanchine: Ballet Master: A Biography*, London: Hamilton

Cage, John (1987) *Silence: Lectures and Writings*, London: Marion Boyars

Caute, David (1988) *The Year of the Barricades: A Journey through 1968*, New York and London: Harper & Row

Coe, Robert (1979) 'Death Destruction and Detroit in Berlin: Robert Wilson's Tale of Two Cities', *Performance Art* 1: 1, pp. 3–7

Copeland, Roger (2004) *Merce Cunningham: The Modernizing of Modern Dance*, London and New York: Routledge

Craig, Edward Gordon (1957) *On the Art of the Theatre*, London: Heinemann

—— (1978) *On Movement and Dance*, ed. Arnold Rood, London: Dance Books

Cunningham, Merce in conversation with Jacqueline Lesschaeve (1991) *The Dancer and the Dance*, London and New York: Marion Boyars

Dawn, Dietrich (1992) 'Space/Time and the Tapestry of Silence: The Quantum Theater of Robert Wilson', *Word & Image* 8: 3, pp. 173–82

Du Vignal, Philippe (1991) 'Bob Wilson – passé, présent, futur: interview par Philippe du Vignal', *Art Press* 163, pp. 12–18

Eco, Umberto (1993) 'Robert Wilson and Umberto Eco: A Conversation', *Performing Arts Journal* 43: 1, pp. 86–96

Enright, Robert (1994) 'A Clean, Well-lighted Grace: An Interview with Robert Wilson', *Border Crossings* 13: 2, pp. 14–22

Fairbrother, Trevor (1991) *Robert Wilson's Vision*, Boston, MA: Museum of Fine Arts in association with Harry N. Abrams, Inc. Publishers, New York

Flakes, Susan (1976) 'Robert Wilson's *Einstein On the Beach*', *The Drama Review*, 20: 4, pp. 69–82

Francis, Richard (1984) *Jasper Johns*, New York: Abbeville

Friedl, Peter (1982) 'Une perception autre: entretien avec Bob Wilson', *Théâtre/Public* 48, pp. 54–9

Fuchs, Elinor (1986) 'The PAJ Casebook: *Alcestis*', *Performing Arts Journal*, 10: 1, pp. 80–105

Glass, Philip (1988) *Opera on the Beach: Philip Glass on His New World of Music Theatre*, London: Faber

Graham, Martha (1991) *Blood Memory*, London: Macmillan

Grillet Thierry and Robert Wilson (1992) 'Wilson selon Wilson', *Theatre/Public* 106, pp. 8–13

Gropius, Walter and Arthur S. Wensinger (ed.) (1961) *The Theatre of the Bauhaus*, Middleton, CT: Wesleyan University Press

Harris, Mary Emma (1987) *The Arts at Black Mountain College*, Cambridge, MA and London: MIT Press

Heale, M.J. (2001) *The Sixties in America: History, Politics and Protest*, Keele: Keele University Press

Holmberg, Arthur (1988) 'A Conversation with Robert Wilson and Heiner Muller', *Modern Drama* 31: 3, pp. 454–8

—— (1996) *The Theatre of Robert Wilson*, Cambridge: Cambridge University Press

Howell, John (1985) 'Forum: What a Legend Becomes', *Artforum International* 23, p. 90

Hughes, Robert (1980) *The Shock of the New: Art and the Century of Change*, London: BBC Books

Huppert, Isabelle (1994) 'Echanges avec Pierre Soulages et Bob Wilson', *Cahiers du Cinéma* 477, pp. 64–8

Ibsen, Henrik (1980) *Peer Gynt*, trans. Peter Watts, Harmondsworth: Penguin Books

I La Galigo (2004) [programme book of the production], Milan: Change Performing Arts

Innes, Christopher (1998) *Edward Cordon Craig: A Vision of Theatre*, Amsterdam: Harwood Academic Publishers

James, Jamie (1996) 'From Lohengrin to Catherine Deneuve', *Art News* 95, pp. 98–102

Jones, Maldwyn A. (1995) *The Limits of Liberty: American History 1607–1992*, Oxford: Oxford University Press

Kaprow, Allan (1966) *Assemblage, Environments and Happenings*, New York: Harry N. Abrams

—— (1967) ' "Happenings" in the New York Scene' in *The Modern American Theater: A Collection of Critical Essays*, ed. Alvin B. Kernan, Englewood Cliffs, NJ: Prentice-Hall, pp. 121–30

Kirstein, Lincoln (ed.) (1984) *Portrait of Mr B*, New York: The Viking Press

Kristeva, Julia (1994) 'Robert Wilson', *ArtPress* 191, pp. 64–5

Langton, Basil (1973) 'Journey to Ka Mountain', *The Drama Review* 17: 2, pp. 48–57

Lawrence, Greg (2002) *Dance with Demons: The Life of Jerome Robbins*, New York: Berkley Books

Lesschaeve, Jacqueline (1977) 'Robert Wilson: résponses', *Tel Quel* No. 71/73, pp. 217–25

Letzler Cole, Susan (1992) *Directors in Rehearsal: A Hidden World*, New York: Routledge

Marranca, Bonnie (ed.) (1996) *The Theatre of Images*, Baltimore, MD: Johns Hopkins University Press

Maurin, Frederic (2001) 'Au Péril de la beauté: la chair du visuel et le cristal de la forme chez Robert Wilson' in *Les Voies de la Création Théâtrale*, ed. Béatrice Picon-Vallin, vol. XXI, Paris: CNRS Editions, pp. 49–69

Meyerhold, Vsevolod (1998) *Meyerhold on Theatre*, ed. Edward Braun, London: Methuen

Morey, Miguel and Carmen Pardo (2003) *Robert Wilson*, Barcelona: Ediciones Poligrafa

Owens, Craig (1978) '*Einstein on the Beach*: The Primacy of Metaphor', *October*, Fall, pp. 21–32

Poling, Clark V. (1986) *Kandinsky's Teaching at the Bauhaus: Color Theory and Analytical Drawing*, New York: Rizzoli

Quadri, Franco (2004) 'The Complete Enchantment', *I La Galigo*, Milan: Change Performing Arts, pp. 69–71

Quadri, Franco, Franco Bertoni and Robert Stearns (1997) *Robert Wilson*, Paris: Editions Plume

Rommen, Ann-Christin (2005) Unpublished interview

Sayre, Henry M. (1989) *The Object of Performance: The American Avant-Garde Since 1970*, Chicago, IL and London: University of Chicago Press

Scanlan, Robert (1995) 'Post-modern Time and Place: Wilson/Müller Intersections', *Art & Design* 10, pp. 76–81

Scarpetta, Guy (1978) 'Bob Wilson. I Was Sitting on My Patio This Guy Appeared I Thought I Was Hallucinating', *Art Press International* 53, pp 30–1

Schechner, Richard (2003) 'Robert Wilson and Fred Newman. A Dialogue on Politics and Therapy, Stillness and Vaudeville', *The Drama Review* 47: 3, pp. 113–28

Shakespeare, William (2005) *The Winter's Tale*, ed. J.H.P. Pafford, London: The Arden Shakespeare

Shank, Theodore (2002) *Beyond the Boundaries: American Alternative Theatre*, Ann Arbor, MI: University of Michigan Press

Shevtsova, Maria (1995a) 'Of "Butterfly" and Men: Robert Wilson Directs Diana Soviero at the Paris Opera', *New Theatre Quarterly* 11: 41, pp. 3–16

—— (1995b) 'Isabelle Huppert Becomes Orlando', *TheatreForum* 6, pp. 69–75

—— (1996) 'A Theatre that Speaks to Citizens: Interview with Ariane Mnouchkine', *Western European Stages* 7: 3, pp. 5–12

—— (1998a) '*La Maladie de la mort*', *Dance Theatre Journal* 14: 1, pp. 31–3

—— (1998b) 'Lucinda Childs and Robert Wilson: *La Maladie de la mort* and Interview with Lucinda Childs', *Western European Stages* 10: 2, pp. 15–24

—— (2001) 'From Swan to Seagull: Modernism in Chekhov and Robert Wilson' in *Matters of the Mind: Poems, Essays and Interviews in Honour of Leonie Kramer*, ed. Lee Jobling and Catherine Runcie, Sydney: University of Sydney Press, pp. 165–175

Shevtsova, Maria (2004) *Dodin and the Maly Drama Theatre: Process to Performance*, London: Routledge

Shyer, Laurence (1985) 'Robert Wilson: *The CIVIL warS* and After', *Theater* 16: 3, pp. 72–80

—— (1989) *Robert Wilson and His Collaborators*, New York: Theatre Communications Group

Simmer, Bill (1976) 'Robert Wilson and Therapy', *The Drama Review* 20: 1, pp. 99–110

Sontag, Susan (1994) *Against Interpretation*, London: Vintage

Stearns, Robert (ed.) (1984) *Robert Wilson: The Theater of Images*, New York: Harper and Row, Publishers

Stein, Gertrude (1993) *Selected Operas & Plays of Gertrude Stein*, ed. John Malcom Brinnin, Pittsburgh: University of Pittsburgh Press

Steiner, Rudolf (1971) *Colour*, trans. John Salter, London: Rudolf Steiner Press

Teschke, Holger (1999) 'Brecht's Learning Plays – a Dance Floor for an Epic Dramaturgy. A Rehearsal Report on Robert Wilson's *Ozeanflug* at the Berliner Ensemble', trans. Joe Compton, *TheatreForum* 14, pp. 10–16

Trilling, Ossia (1973) 'Robert Wilson's *Ka Mountain and Guardenia Terrace*', *The Drama Review* 17: 2, pp. 33–47

Tytell, John (1997) *The Living Theatre: Art, Exile, and Outrage*, London: Methuen

Vanden Heuvel, Michael (1993) *Performing Drama / Dramatizing Performance: Alternative Theater and the Dramatic Text*, Ann Arbor, MI: University of Michigan Press

Whitford, Frank (1984) *Bauhaus*, London: Thames and Hudson

Wilmeth, Don B. and Christopher Bigsby (eds) (2002) *The Cambridge History of American Theatre, Volume Three: Post-World War II to the 1990s*, Cambridge: Cambridge University Press

Wilson, Robert (1977a) 'A Letter for Queen Victoria' in *The Theatre of Images*, ed. Bonnie Marranca, Baltimore, MD and London: Johns Hopkins University Press, pp. 50–109

—— (1977b) '. . . I thought I was hallucinating', *The Drama Review* 21: 4, pp. 75–8

—— (1979) 'I Was Sitting on My Patio This Guy Appeared I Thought I Was Hallucinating', *Performing Arts Journal* 4, pp. 200–18

—— (1992) 'A propos de *Dr Faustus Lights the Lights*,' *Theatre/Public* 106, pp. 54–60

—— (1997) Preface to *Strehler dirige: Le tesi di un allestimento e l'impulso musicale nel teatro*, ed. Giancarlo Stampalia, Venice: Marsilio Editori, pp. 11–16

—— (2002) 'Robert Wilson: Interview', *The Twentieth Century Performance Reader*, ed. Michael Huxley and Noel Witts, London and New York: Routledge, pp. 420–33

—— (2005) 'Bob Wilson and *The Ring*: Painting with Light' [Interview with Franck Mallet], *ArtPress* 316, pp. 47–51

VIDEOGRAPHY

Brookner, Howard (1985) *Robert Wilson and the CIVIL warS*, Aspekt Telefilm-Produktion

Brookner, Howard and Charles Chabot (1985) *The Theatre of Robert Wilson*, BBC

Figgis, Mike (1998) *H.G.: Robert Wilson and Hans-Peter Kuhn in London, 1895–1985*, Artangel

Kessel, Marion (1992–93) *Robert Wilson x 2+: Visions of Robert Wilson*, Arts Alive Productions

—— (1995) *The Making of a Monologue. Robert Wilson's* Hamlet, Arts Alive/Caddell and Conwell Foundation for the Arts

Obenhaus, Mark (1985) *Einstein on the Beach: The Changing Image of Opera*, Obenhaus Films/Brooklyn Academy of Music

Pegram, Lorna (1980) *The Shock of the New, 7, Culture as Nature*, BBC/RM Arts

DISCOGRAPHY

Glass, Philip/Robert Wilson (1979) *Einstein on the Beach*, CBS Masterworks

Glass, Philip/Robert Wilson and Maita di Niscemi (1999) *The CIVIl warS: A Tree Is Best Measured When It Is Down, Act V — The Rome Section*, Nonesuch

Waits, Tom (1993) *The Black Rider*, Island Records Inc.

—— (2002) *Blood Money* [lyrics for *Woyzeck*], Anti Inc.

INDEX

Note: Page numbers in **bold** refer to figures.

4'33" 17

abstract expressionism 15
actor 32, 57–63; workshop 48–50; *see also* performers
adaptations from prose 32–3
'Against Interpretation' 17
Aida 54, 92, 105
Alcestis 25, 31, 36
Alice 10, 36
Alice in Bed 33, 36
Alley Cats 6
allusion 27, 29, 34, 78, 90, 97, 113, 114, 116, 150
America Hurrah 4
American Repertory Theatre (ART) 31
American Theater Laboratory 4
Anderson, Laurie 25, 31
Anderson Theatre 7
Andrews, Raymond 10
animal sounds 136–8
Anthroposophy 15
Appia, Adolphe 54, 63, 64
Aragon, Louis 9

architecture 2, 42, 63, 80, 89, 104; in space 52–6; in time 52–3, 56–7
Arens, Katherine 29
Armani, Giorgio 3
Aronson, Arnold 25, 26
art and politics 14–26; finance and formalism 22–6
Artaud, Antonin 14
artificial acting 58
artist 8, 16, 20, 26, 37–8, 86
'art of the actor' 43
'art of the text' 43
assemblage 46, 140
'astonishing modern-day mystery play' 86
atmosphere 32, 55, 64, 65, 102, 126, 138, 139, 151
audience 5, 6, 13, 14, 18, 29, 51, 56, 63, 65, 67, 68, 93, 97, 102, 109, 114, 131, 137, 150
Autumn Festival 84, 88
avant-garde 4–5, 24, 36, 38, 54, 84, 89, 131
Avignon Festival 18, 83

Baby 5
Bach, Johann Sebastian 91, 109
Balanchine, George 16
Bali Purnati Centre for the
    Arts 39
ballet *see* dancing
Banes, Sally 88
Baraka, Amiri 20
Barnes, Clive 85
Bauhaus 15, 103–4
Bayrak, Libe 5
Beat generation 19
beauty 56, 77
Beck, Julian 6, 18
Bentzen, Sverre 71
Berliner Ensemble 33, 49
Bertoni, Franco 95
Betty Nansen Theatre 36
Bigsby, Christopher 19
Black Mountain College 14, 15
Black Power groups 20
The Black Rider 19, 36, 37, 57, 65, **66**,
    77, 78, 80, 82, 105, 132, 138
Blood Money 141
body imaging 129–31, 149
body/movement 76–8; *see also*
    movement
Boulez, Pierre 14
Bread and Puppet Theatre 25
breathing 122–3, 138
Brecht, Bertolt 48, 49, 51
Brecht, Stefan 1, 2, 5, 105, 109,
    113, 115
Brennan, Kathleen 36, 67
Breton, André 9
Brook, Peter 32, 41, 71
Brooklyn Academy of Music (BAM) 7,
    86, 88, 108
Brookner, Howard 29
Brown, Trisha 17, 24
Bryars, Gavin 31
Büchner, Georg 67, 70, 72
Burroughs, William 19, 37
Bush, George 21
Byrd Hoffman Foundation,
    Inc. 7
ByrdwoMAN 6

The Cabinet of Dr Calagari 38
Cage, John 6, 14, 15, 17, 18, 132
camp 34, 60, 105, 132, 138
canvas 15, 16, 27, 53, 112
Cardin, Pierre 13
Carmen 141
Carroll, Lewis 36
Carter, Jimmy 21
casting 10, 12, 29, 48, 80
Caute, David 19
Cézanne, Paul 53, 54, 112
Chaikin, Joseph 25
Chaplin, Charlie 57, 128
character 6, 7, 58, 59, 60, 65, 68, 73,
    77, 78, 80, 116, 132, 149
Charpentier, Marc-Antoine 36
Châtelet Theatre 36, 38
Chekhov, Anton 33, 35
Chekhov, Michael 120
Chéreau, Patrice 32
Childs, Lucinda 13, 16, 18, 32, 87
choreography 31, 48, 84, 87, 109, 126,
    129; *see also* dancing
chorus 91, 93, 95, 99, 104
the CIVIL warS 27, 29–30, 31, 36, 46, 85
Cold War 19, 21
Coles, Honni 57
collage 29, 71, 112–13, 140, 144
colour 1, 15, 16, 27, 46, 59, 60, 63–9,
    98, 112, 140, 149
coloured light 65–9
Comédie Française 60, 63
comic 11, 57, 60, 111, 128, 132, 136
composition 5, 6, 14–15, 17, 26, 33,
    48, 53, 84, 89, 121, 128, 129, 132–3,
    135, 138; *see also* music
conservatism 21, 83
constructivism 98, 99–100, 103,
    116, 154
content 5, 17, 27, 47, 74, 77, 89, 92–3,
    103, 115, 116, 117, 144
continuity principle 73
contrast 29, 37, 100, 121–2, 124–6,
    130, 134
Co-op 6
Copeland, Roger 1
costumes 78–80, 82, 95, 129

counterpoint 53, 56, 67, 73–4, 78, 99, 140–1, 142
court opera 36
Covent Garden 92
Craig, Edward Gordon 52, 54, 57, 58, 59, 78, 131
'Crazy Eddie' 97
creative tension 52
cubism 112, 116, 154
culture 14, 16, 18, 22, 23, 29, 30, 37, 38, 68, 88, 112–13
'culture for everybody' 39
Cunningham, Merce 6, 14, 18, 53
Curious George 13
cyclorama 65, 67, 68, 82, 95, 97, 106

Dada 154
dancing 1, 12, 16, 17, 42, 43, 46, 48, 51, 56, 68, 89, 98, 102, 105, 106, 111, 113, 126, 127, 128, 129, 140; *see also* choreography
Danton's Death 35
Deafman Glance 8, 9, 82, 83
Death Destruction and Detroit 27–9, 46
Death Destruction and Detroit II 31
Death Destruction and Detroit III 13
Debussy, Claude 55–6
'decorative task' 77
de Groat, Andy 5, 87
de Quincey, Thomas 37
Description of a Picture 31
designing 12, 47, 54, 76, 77–8, 82, 125
Despoiled Shore Media Material Landscape with Argonauts 31
Det Norske Teatret 47, 74
Dia Log 13
dialogue 47, 49, 71, 72, 74, 139, 148, 149
Die Freischütz (The Free-Shooter) 37
di Niscemi, Maita 27
director 35, 38, 63, 143
dislocated history 26–32
distance 59, 76, 78, 80, 125, 131, 136
Doctor Faustus Lights the Lights 4
Dostoevsky, Fyodor 33
drama classics 33–6
dramaturg 32–3, 47–9, 50, 67, 72, 74

dramaturgical intervention 143–9
Dream Play 71
Duchamp, Marcel 14
Duras, Marguerite 32

Eco, Umberto 58, 70
Edinburgh Festival 32
Edison, Thomas 27
efficiency 50, 142
Einstein, Albert 85, 89–90, 91, 95, 97, 98, 99, 100, 103, 105, 106, 108–9, 111, 114, 116, 117
Einstein on the Beach 22, 42, 83; Act 1/ Scene 1/Train 1 94–8; Act 1/ Scene 2/Trial 1 98–100; Act 2/ Scene 1/Field 1 100–2; Act 2/ Scene 2/Train 2 102–3; Act 3/ Scene 1/Trial 2 103–6; Act 3/ Scene 2/Field 2 106; Act 4/Scene 1/ Train 3 109; Act 4/Scene 2/Trial 3 109–10; Act 4/Scene 3/Field 3 110–11; itinerary and reception 83–8; Knee Play 1 93–4; Knee Play 2 100; Knee Play 3 103; Knee Play 4 106–9; Knee Play 5 111–12; landmark 88–9; structure and form 89–92
Elsinore 71
El Teatro Campesino 20, 25
emotion 15, 60, 63, 67, 68, 76, 92, 116–17, 127, 140
Enright, Robert 42, 59, 60, 63, 70
expressionism 153, 154, 154–5
exterior screen 114, 115

Faithfull, Marianne 37
The Fatal Marksman 37
Febers, Jutta 146
field theme 90, 100, 106, 110, 113
'fill in the form' principle 58–9, 71, 120
Flakes, Susan 104
folk-rock music 36–8
Foreman, Richard 8, 25, 26
The Forest 32
Fosse, Jon 74
Four Saints in Three Acts 12

Francis, Richard 17
Frederick the Great 27
Freud, Sigmund 7–8, 54, 78, 82
Friedl, Peter 22, 41, 46, 70
Fuchs, Elinor 76

Galasso, Michael 46
Garibaldi, Guiseppe 27
Garnier theatre, Paris 39
garments 78, 80, 130
Gelber, Jack 18
German expressionism 154–5
Gesamtkunstwerk 12–13
gesture 12, 46, 53, 63, 78, 92, 99, 112,
    129; gestural language 43–6; *see also*
    visual book
Ginsberg, Allen 19
Giscard d'Estaing, Valéry 23
Glass, Philip 13, 84, 87, 89, 90,
    91, 92, 114
Gluck, Christophe Willibald 36
'God's Away on Business' 70
THE GODS ARE POUNDING MY HEAD
    (AKA Lumberjack Messiah) 26
Goethe, Johann Wolfgang von 15, 42
Graham, Martha 1
grand opera 36, 38
Grillet, Thierry 16, 48, 64
Gropius, Walter 16, 104
grotesque 76–8
Grotowski, Jerzy 92, 116
Guildenstern 131, 150
Guillem, Sylvie 63
Gulf War 21
Gussow, Mel 85
Guy, Michel 13

Haft Tan Mountain 10
Hamlet 33–4, 54, 64, 71, 78, 131,
    141, 149
Hamletmachine 31
Hanayagi, Suzushi 31, 43
Hansberry, Lorraine 20
'Happenings' 6
Harris, Mary Emma 14
Heale, M.J. 19, 20
Hearst, Patty 104

Hess, Rudolf 27, 28
Hoffman, Byrd 1, 4, 6–7, 26
Holmberg, Arthur 53, 54, 56, 57, 58,
    63, 87–8, 113, 114
Hoppe, Marianne 33, 63
Howell, John 87
Hughes, Robert 5
Huppert, Isabelle 32, 59, 89, 95, 130

Ibsen, Henrik 35, 54, 72, 81, 146
I Ching 14–15
I La Galigo 39, 40, 43, **44**, **45**
image 16, 27, 28, 29, 34, 72–3, 76,
    102, 109, 129–31, 141, 149–50
imagination 3, 6, 27, 32, 93, 119, 134
incongruity 31, 56, 105, 130
Inland Revenue Service 18
Innes, Christopher 54
interior acting style 58
interior reflection *see* interior screen
interior screen 56, 71, 114, 128
International Art Fair 13
*I Was Sitting on My Patio This Guy Appeared I
    Thought I was Hallucinating* 18, 121

Johns, Jasper 16, 92
Johnson, Samuel 87, 91, 99
Jones, LeRoi 20
Jones, Maldwyn A. 19, 20
Jones, Robert T. 84
Judd, Donald 15
Judson Dance Theatre 16
Junk Dances 4
juxtaposition 56, 67, 112, 114, 130

Kabuki 43, 131
KA MOUNTAIN and GUARDenia TERRACE
    10, **11**, 13
Kandinsky, Wassily 15
Kantor, Tadeusz 41
Kaprow, Allan 6
Keaton, Buster 57, 128
Kennedy, John F. 20
King, Kenneth 5, 12
King, Martin Luther 20
King Lear 33, 63
The King of Spain 7, 115

Kirstein, Lincoln 16
Knee Plays 90, 93, 100, 103, 106, 111, 112
Knowles, Christopher 11, 12, 13, 91, 99
Kristeva, Julia 3
Kuhn, Hans Peter 3, 33, 136

The Lady from the Sea 35
La Fontaine, Jean de 35–6, 60, 73
La Maladie de la mort 32, 33, 80, 136
Lampe, Jutta 32
Lang, Fritz 98
Lang, Jack 9, 39
language 11, 31, 32, 43, 70, 73, 74, 135
La Scala 35
Lautréamont 56
Lawrence, Greg 4
layering 97, 98, 112, 133, 136
LeCompte, Elizabeth 25
Lecoq, Jacques 120
Lee, Robert E. 27
Le Martyre de Saint-Sébastien 63
Lepage, Robert 71
Les Fables de La Fontaine 60, **61**, 63, 77
Lesschaeve, Jacqueline 1, 52, 92, 116
A Letter for Queen Victoria 11–14, 84
letters and words 139
Letzler Cole, Susan 73
The Life And Times of Joseph Stalin 9, 46
The Life and Times of Sigmund Freud 7
light 50, 63–9, 77–8, 86, 97, 102, 106, 116, 129, 151–2
Lincoln, Abraham 27
The Little Prince 33
Living Theatre 6, 18, 92, 116
Louis, Murray 4
Lyon Opéra 36

Mabou Mines 25, 89, 108
McCarthyism 19
McNeil, George 2
Madama Butterfly 64, 65
Maeterlinck, Maurice 56
The Magic Flute 38, 39
make-up 60, 131–2, 137

The Making of a Monologue: Robert Wilson's Hamlet 127
Malevich, Kasimir 15
Malina, Judith 6, 18
Maly Drama Theatre of St Petersburg 46
Marranca, Bonnie 12
masks 60–3, 76, 130, 131
Medea 31
Médeé 36
The Meek Girl 33, 74
Memory / Loss 3
Metropolis 98
Metropolitan Opera 84, 85, 92
Meyerhold, Vsevolod 50, 77, 78, 103
Minimalism 16–17, 76, 89
mise en scène 31, 55, 144
'Misery is The River of the World' 70
Mitterrand, François 9, 39
Mnouchkine, Ariane 43
modernism 15, 50, 52, 103
Moholy-Nagy, Laszlo 16
Moholy-Nagy, Sybil 16
Molière, Jean-Baptiste 42
Monk, Meredith 6
Monogram 4–5
Monsters of Grace 36
Morey, Miguel 16, 43
Moscow Art Theatre 54
movement 1, 5, 16, 31, 33, 37, 47, 50, 51, 53, 56, 68, 72, 76–8, 89, 92, 93, 94, 99, 100, 104, 112, 121–9, 130, 140, 149; breathing 122–3; contrasts in 124–6; score 50, 128–9; variations in 127–8; walking 123–4; *see also* body / movement
Mozart, Wolfgang Amadeus 38
Müller, Heiner 31–2, 35, 48, 49
Munch, Edvard 76
music 13, 24–5, 31, 56, 73–4, 76, 91, 111, 133, 140–2; *see also* composition
music theatre 36–40, 84

The Naked Lunch 19
Nancy Festival 8–9
National Endowment for the Arts 22, 23
National Paris Opera 39
natural sounds 136

neo-dadaist movement 14
Newnam, Barnett 15–16
Next Wave Festival 86
Nikolais, Alwin 4
Nixon, Richard 21, 22, 24
Noah's Ark 10
Noh 29, 43, 131
noise 17, 102

Obenhaus, Mark 53, 56, 57, 112
objects 17, 24, 36, 80–2, 129
Odéon Theatre 18
oeuvre 36, 73, 82, 149
Ohlsson, Monica 46, 47, 50, 144, 146
Oklahoma 38
Olympic Arts Festival, Los Angeles 29, 30, 86
Ontological-Hysteric Theatre 8
Open Theatre 25
Opéra Bastille 38, 39
Orlando 32, 33, 36, 59, **82**
Orphée et Euridyce 36
Overture for a Deafman 9–10, 13
Ozeanflug (Oceanflight) 49, 50

painter 15–16, 76
Paradise Now 18
paralinguistics 133, 138–9
Pardo, Carmen 16, 43
Paris Opera 39, 63
Parmeggiani, Frida 78
Peacock Theatre 32
Peer Gynt 35, 46, 47, 50, 51, 54, **55**, 60, **62**, 71, 72, 73, 74, **75**, 82, 136, 137
Pegram, Lorna 5
Pelléas and Mélisande 55–6
performers 5–7, 47, 51, 57, 59, 63, 87, 105, 116; *see also* actor
Piccoli, Michel 32
POEtry 36, 37
Poles 2, 5
Pompidou, Georges Jean Raymond 23
postmodernism 52, 155–6
practical exercises 119; body imaging 129–31; light 151–2; make-up 131–2; movement 121–9; music 140–2; silent play composing 132–3;

sound 133–9; texts, working with 142–50
presentation 31, 57–8, 144
production themes 112
proscenium 7, 53–4
prose adaptations 32–3
Puccini's score 65

Quadri, Franco 51, 95
Quartett 31

Racine, Jean 42
Rafaelsen, Henrick 72
Rakha, Alla 91
Rauschenberg, Robert 4, 14, 15
Reagan, Ronald 21–2
Reed, Lou 37
resonance 17, 67, 74, 114, 137
Restu, I. Kusumaningrum 51–2
reverberation 71, 73, 137, 139
Reynaud, Jacques 60, 78
rhythm 32, 36, 50, 57, 64, 74, 83, 87, 91, 95, 110, 112, 128, 134
Richardson, Miranda 32
Ring 38, 76; *see also* Wagner
Robbins, Jerome 4, 7, 84
Rockwell, John 86, 110
Rommen, Ann-Christin 46, 48–9, 51, 67, 71
Roof Piece 17, 24
Rosencrantz 131, 150

Saint-Exupéry, Antoine de 33
Saints and Singing 12
Salomé 35
San Francisco Mime Troupe 20–1
Sayre, Henry M. 24
Schaeffer, Pierre 14
Schaubühne am Lehniner Platz 23, 27, 31, 32, 33
Schechner, Richard 6, 56–7, 58, 59, 135
Schiller, Johann von 42
Schlemmer, Oscar 103–4
School of Byrds 6–7
score 37, 50, 55, 59, 65, 74, 85, 91, 134; movement score 128–9
screams 76

screen 29, 54, 56
sculpture 2–3, 80, 109
Shakespeare, William 147, 148
Shank, Theodore 18, 20–1, 25
Shankar, Ravi 91
Shevtsova, Maria 43, 46, 59
Shiraz Festival 10
Shyer, Laurence 4, 6, 9, 27, 28, 29, 30, 32, 41, 54, 84, 85, 89, 92, 108
'significant content' 116
silence 7, 9, 10, 17, 73–7, 106, 121, 132, 141
Silence 17
'silent majority' 21
silent operas 7–14, 60, 73, 78
silent play 48–9, 51; composing of 132–3
The Silent Scream (canvas) 76
Soleri, Paolo 2
solo score 59
sonority 73, 135, 139; *see also* sound
Sontag, Susan 17, 33, 35
sound 1, 10, 11, 33, 36, 72, 73–7, 91, 94, 112; animal sounds 136–8; found sounds 134–6; letters and words 139; natural sounds 136; paralinguistics 133, 138–9
space 2, 7–8, 15, 34, 42, 47, 52–5, 59, 63, 64–5, 68, 76, 90, 100, 103, 104, 113, 121, 123, 125
spaceship themes 90, 110, 112, 113
spectators *see* audience
speech 24, 78, 87, 103, 105, 112, 134, 146, 149
Split Britches 25
Star Wars 78
Stearns, Robert 2, 17, 95
Stein, Gertrude 4, 12
Stein, Peter 27
Steiner, Rudolf 15
Stop the Draft Week 21
Strauss, Richard 35
Strehler, Giorgio 63
Strindberg, August 35, 71
structure 32, 37, 47, 53, 54, 59, 69, 87, 89, 91, 93, 129, 138, 141, 154
subtext 58, 60

Sureq Galigo 39, 40
surrealism 9, 15, 109, 115, 130–1
Surrealist Manifesto 9
Sutherland, Joan 92, 105
Sutton, Sheryl 13, 87, 94, 100, 103, 104, 113
Swan Song 33

table workshop 47–8
tango 68, 78
Terry, Megan 25
Teschke, Holger 49, 50–1, 63, 134
text 3, 35, 47, 48, 50–1, 67, 70–3, 74, 80, 100, 135, 143, 144–5, 147, 149–50
textured arrangement 12, 50
Thalia Theatre 31, 36
Theatre Activity 1 5
Theatre Activity 2 6
The Theatre and its Double 14
Theatre Piece 1 14
theme 29, 33, 90, 112, 113, 126, 133; *see also individual entries*
Thomson, Virgil 12
The Threepenny Opera 38
Three Sisters 10, 35, 46
time 7–8, 34, 42, 46, 50, 52–3, 56–7, 63, 64, 65, 90, 103, 113, 128, 150
Time Rocker 36, 37
torch dance 87, 111
train theme 90, 94, 97, 102, 112, 113
'trance' 57–8, 104, 126
trial theme 90, 98, 103, 104, 105–6, 109, 112

Übermarionette 57

Vanden Heuvel, Michael 115
Van Itallie, Jean-Claude 4
vaudeville 12, 34, 38, 57, 127, 128, 132
Venice Biennale 2, 84
Vietnam War 5, 21
Viet Rock 25
visual book 42–6, 54, 71, 72; method 142–3; *see also* gesture

Wagner, Richard 12, 38, 54
Waits, Tom 36, 37, 67, 70, 141
walking 94, 123–4, 125, 126, 142
Warhol, Andy 24
Warrilow, David 108
Watergate 21, 24
Watermill Centre 23, 119–2
Weber, Carl Maria von 38
Weill, Kurt 37, 38
Wensinger, Arthur S. 103–4
When We Dead Awaken 57
Wiens, Wofgang 67, 144
Williams, Tennessee 42
Wilmeth, Don B. 19

Wilson, Robert 16, 48, 54, 56, 63, 64,
   69, 121
The Wind and the Reed 73
Wings on Rock 33
The Winter's Tale 33, 78, 80, **81**, 146
The Wizard of Oz 78
Wold, Susse 32
Woolf, Virginia 32
Wooster Group 25–6
workshop method: from storyboard to
   visual book 42–6; workshops 46–52
Woyzeck 36, 67–9, 70, 72, 77–8, **79**, 105

Zurich Opera 38

Theatre Histories:
An Introduction

Edited by Philip B. Zarrilli, Bruce McConahie, Gary Jay Williams and Carol Fisher Sorgenfrei

'This book will significantly change theatre education'
Janelle Reinelt, *University of California, Irvine*

Theatre Histories: An Introduction is a radically new way of looking at both the way history is written and the way we understand performance.

The authors provide beginning students and teachers with a clear, exciting journey through centuries of Eurpoean, North the South American, African and Asian forms of theatre and performance.

Challenging the standard format of one-volume theatre history texts, they help the reader think critically about this vibrant field through fascinating yet plain-speaking essays and case studies.

Among the topics covered are:

- representation and human expression
- interpretation and critical approaches
- historical method and sources
- communication technologies
- colonization
- oral and literate cultures
- popular, sacred and elite forms of performance.

Keeping performance and culture very much centre stage, *Theatre Histories: An Introduction* is compatible with standard play anthologies, full of insightful pedagogical apparatus, and comes accompanied by web site resources.

ISBN Hb: 978–0–415–22727–8
ISBN Pb: 978–0–415–22728–5